Repercussions

My Sister's Story

Vaughan Earle Justice

LYSTRA BOOKS
& Literary Services

ISBN 979-8-9850083-7-1 paperback
ISBN 979-8-9850083-8-8 ebook
Library of Congress Control Number: 2023912823

An earlier version of *Repercussions* was independently published in 2017.

"Nostaligia" is quoted by the kind permission of the poet Dawn Potter and publisher Deerbrook Editions, Cumberland, Maine.

Author's photograph by Gabrielle Shain.

Book design by Kelly Prelipp Lojk.

LYSTRA BOOKS
&: Literary Services

Published by Lystra Books & Literary Services, LLC
391 Lystra Estates Drive
Chapel Hill, NC 27517
lystrabooks@gmail.com

For John and Sophie—and for me

Rick, Mom, and Lind, 1944, in Lynchburg, Virginia.

AUTHOR'S NOTE

This memoir about my older sister, Lind, is a work of creative nonfiction. In it I have tried to piece together the relationships and experiences she had in her life, so that I might answer the many questions I have about its trajectory.

These events are portrayed to the best of my memory and the accounts of those who kindly shared their memories with me. This is the story as I tell it and may not be exactly as it happened.

Included are a number of letters and emails from friends and relatives whose lives are part of the story. In most cases I have retained the original spelling and punctuation in hopes of showing their personalities, as well as their words.

—Vaughan Justice

Repercussions—unintended, unhappy consequences that can occur after an event or action.

The call came in late November 2009. I was married, the mother of two, living in Charlotte, North Carolina, and working as executive producer in a commercial-film production company.

"Is this Vaughan Earle Justice?"

"Yesss," I answered, wary it might be a caller wanting an acting job or promoting a movie script.

"I am Karen Garraputa of post-adoption services for the Children's Home Society of North Carolina. Some important adoption laws have recently changed, and your sister's birth son wants to meet his family."

"I'm sorry. What did you say again?" Surely I had misunderstood her.

"Your sister had a son and gave him up for adoption," Karen said. "His name is John Davis. He has already found his birth father and met with him."

My mind was racing. Lind had a son. Did I hear correctly? When did this happen? My heart was beating in my throat.

"His father still lives in Salisbury, so he was easy to find," Karen said. "But finding your sister has been much harder. No family member on your side is still living in town. John hopes to meet you, but I need to get your permission for him to contact you."

I thought I might cry. My voice was shaky when I answered.

"Yes. Please have him contact me. That would be wonderful. I would love to hear from him."

My sister had a son. I don't remember anything else Karen said. Something about emailing. I was in shock. I had more questions, so many more questions, but could not formulate one into words at that moment.

When we hung up, I could hardly breathe. I called my husband, Don, who worked from home.

"Wow," Don said, "that must have been who called last week asking if I would give them Lind's address."

"You didn't think to tell me?"

"Well, I was in my office working. I was really busy, and that's all she asked. I gave her your work number. I figured she'd call you. Sorry, I forgot all about it. Can we talk later? I have another call coming in on my business line."

There was no way I was going to get any more work done. Karen Garraputa's call and the questions I had were all I could think of. I called one of my good friends. She urged caution. "This John Davis may need a kidney."

I ignored her comment. All I knew was, I wanted to find out more about my sister's son. Where had he been? Why didn't I know about him before now? Why didn't Mom tell me? Why didn't Lind tell me? I wished she were here so I could ask her what had happened.

Each day after high school, my sister came home, shut herself in her bedroom, put on a record—jazz, classical music, or opera—and studied while eating seedless green grapes and potato sticks from a can. I was five years old, and I wanted so badly to be in that room with her. I danced and sang in front of the tall pier mirror that stood in the hall just outside her room, hoping Lind would invite me in. She hardly ever did.

There are so few memories I have of my sister when I was young because of the twelve-year age difference. I know she loved music and had stacks of records that were always playing in her room. I know she liked peas and rice, which I like too—maybe because of her. I know she was always well-dressed and good-looking. I could see that.

My family life was a life with Mom and Dad. It was almost like I was an only child. Lind and my brother Rick, twelve and nine years older than me, were never home. Rick was at football practice, on a date, or out with his buddies. He came home from school and headed up to his attic bedroom with a quart of milk and two baloney sandwiches. I might see him later at dinner. Lind was with her girlfriends or involved in after-school activities. I loved my big brother, but I wanted to be just like my sister.

Lind did sometimes let me watch her dress for a date. Her records would be playing, and I would lie on my stomach on her bed or sit on the floor—chattering away, I'm sure. Then the doorbell would ring, Lind would grab one last thing, and run to the front door. I would jump up and run after her so I could catch a glimpse of her as she yelled bye to our parents and left with some handsome guy.

While she was out one night, I sneaked in her room to look through the scrapbook she kept under her bed. In it were lots of newspaper clippings of a football player taped to the pages with hearts she had drawn next to those

*At left, Lind. At right, Mom, Lind, Rick, Dad, and me,
Easter 1955.*

clippings. From my five-year-old's perspective, I thought
she had to be in love.

Until Karen's call about John Davis's existence, I had no
reason to think about Lind's high school boyfriend. I did
not even remember his name. When I learned about John,
I wanted to reconstruct as much as I could of Lind's past.

Soon I found out, John's father was Jim Rabon. He was
the guy in Lind's scrapbook. He and Lind began dating her
freshman year in 1951 and continued dating off and on until Jim graduated in June of 1954.

When I came across Lind's scrapbook again years later, I
realized it offered proof of Lind's affection for Jim. It was a
chronicle of their romance. I had always thought of my sister as being a grown-up, even when she was in high school.

But decades later, her scrapbook shows me the giddy, infatuated teenager she was, just like I had been when I was her age. There were Lind's notes, pictures, and souvenirs from the many things she and Jim had done. On Lind's birthday in September of 1952, Jim and another couple came to our parents' home to celebrate with a birthday dinner before going to the youth center, a favorite hangout. A couple of months later, they attended a dance together. On December 29, they went to a formal "Senior Superlative Night" at the Salisbury Country Club.

For New Year's Eve, 1953, Jim, Lind, and friends drove to Greensboro to celebrate at the Plantation Supper Club, which advertised itself as "the hottest spot between New York and Miami." In February of that year, they attended the school's Valentine dance. When Jim went hunting, he brought her back a squirrel tail. It looks like she had taped it in the scrapbook. There was a stain where it had been— for a short time anyway.

In early summer of 1953, Lind went to Kanuga, an Episcopal church retreat in Hendersonville, and Jim wrote her twice. She put several exclamation points after the word twice in the scrapbook. Her first-place ribbon for a hundred-yard relay was next to the note. There were hayrides at the youth center, 3-D movies, dates, and dancing—seemingly endless weekend nights of being together. Lind went to the Methodist church with Jim and glued the bulletin onto the same page as a napkin with the Rabon name printed on it.

The scrapbook continued into the summer with a trip to the Charlotte Armory for a dance with Johnny Ace's orchestra, featuring Willie Mae "Hound Dog" Thornton. I had to check her out on YouTube. The song was her only hit, four years before Elvis recorded it. And boy could she belt it out.

Lind and twelve girlfriends went to Myrtle Beach for a week, and of course, boys followed. She wrote, "I date Jim every night." She also noted, "We all cook, get tan, feed the boys, don't sleep, have fun, don't want to leave."

It seems to me Lind and Jim were the definition of "going steady" during most of their high school years.

I found a letter from the Eagle Pencil Company in her scrapbook. At the time they offered a handwriting interpretation for ten cents. Lind must have sent a sample of her handwriting in because the letter provided an analysis: My sister had an independent spirit and was not afraid to try out new ideas. She was interested in various activities and her original thoughts and resourcefulness enabled her to adapt to any situation.

The letter continued, "While your manner may seem aloof when you meet people for the first time, you have a vital personality, a romantic heart, and you enjoy being with others. In choosing your intimate friends you are critical."

She paid a good price for things because she wanted only the best, and when the occasion demanded it, she could be most diplomatic.

It seemed Lind's handwriting pretty much gave her away.

At this point in her life, nothing slowed my sister down. Jim Rabon graduated Boyden High School in 1954, a year ahead of her.

Shortly after graduation, Jim left Salisbury for the army and Germany. I am sure Lind and he wrote each other, at least occasionally. She must have missed having him around, but Lind made the most of her senior year in both academics and social life.

Under Lind's senior-year photo in the Boyden High yearbook, the caption read: *She is capable of imagining all, of arranging all, and of doing everything.*

I always believed that about her too.

The sister I adored had a fun-filled, busy life. I can find evidence of her academic accomplishments, her high school years as a cheerleader, the plays she acted in, her time as business manager of the school paper, her popularity. Mom would sometimes tell me about things Lind had done. From all that, I really thought I knew who Lind was, and that was that. But after receiving the phone call about her son's existence, I wondered if I ever really knew her at all.

What would make Lind give up a child? The parents I knew would have loved to have had a grandson. Or were they the ones who made her give him up? Why didn't Mom and I talk about it when I was older, when I believed we were so close? I must admit I was hurt about that, but I didn't sulk. Instead, I began a search to find out more about my sister and her hidden life.

— 2 —

My sister, born in 1937, was named for our mother, Rosalind Johnson, and was called Lind. Seventeen months later, my brother, Gordon Merrick Earle, Jr., was born. He was named after Dad and was known as Rick. Both of my siblings were born in Lynchburg, Virginia, where Dad worked for Firestone Tire and, later, Equitable Life Insurance.

Then Japan bombed Pearl Harbor in December of 1941 and the United States entered the war. In August of 1942, Dad was ordered to report to San Francisco for duty as a lieutenant in the navy. He spent most of the war years on the USS *San Diego* in the Pacific. Mom and other wives and moth-

Dad in his navy uniform.

ers she knew in Lynchburg spent those years taking care of their children and worrying about their husbands.

In December 1943, Mom's twenty-seven-year-old brother, Markus William Johnson III, was killed when his merchant marine ship was blown up off Bari, Italy. Mom took
Lind and Rick to stay with her parents in Savannah, Georgia, for several months. Bessie Kathryn was fifty, and Blake-
ly Hollinshead Johnson was sixty-nine. Mark's name, along
with those of thirteen other young men who were killed in
the war, is inscribed on a marble tablet placed on the south
wall of Christ Church in Savannah.

Mom became anxious and fearful that Dad could be
killed too. Her doctor told her not to listen to the radio or
read the newspaper.

When the war ended, Dad returned to Lynchburg. Not
long afterward his father asked him to come to Salisbury,
North Carolina, to help him in his business, Earle's Office
Supplies. My parents loved living in Lynchburg, but Dad,
an only child, had great respect for his father and mother,
so he acquiesced.

After the horrors of the war, family became everything.

Dad's parents, Isabella and Edwin, whom we called Bam
and Pop, bought the house next door to theirs on Marsh
Street for my parents. It might have been a little too close
for Mom, living next to her in-laws. Bam was a horsewom-
an, a devout Christian Scientist, and one of the few wom-
en of the time who golfed, winning trophies at Pinehurst.
She bought and sold antiques and had, with a few other
college friends, founded the Sigma Sigma Sigma Sorority. I believe Mom was a little intimidated by her and her
accomplishments.

But for Rick and Lind, and then me, it couldn't have
been more wonderful. Our grandparents owned an empty

lot to the right of their house, and it became the neighbor-hood ballfield and playground.

I was born at Rowan Hospital in Salisbury on April 7, 1949. Mom said I was their "after-the-war" baby. Mom was thirty-eight, so I imagine I came as a shock to Rick, nine years old, and Lind, twelve.

The summer of 1955, after Lind graduated high school, our family stayed in Sullivan's Island, South Carolina, for a few weeks. Dad was there for navy reserve duty, and Mom, Rick, Lind, and I were there for fun. Wyndham Robertson, a high school girlfriend of Lind's, asked her friend Robert Wilson who was from nearby Charleston, if he would take Lind out on a date. He agreed. Lind and Robert had a great time together and dated several times those two weeks. But that seemed to be all there was. He was going back to Princeton, and she was headed to college in Virginia. Interestingly though, a connection with Robert years later would have him playing detective for me.

In September 1955, Lind left home to attend Sullins College, a two-year liberal arts women's college in Bris-tol, Virginia. She was soon elected vice president of her class and joined the Sullins Players. Her classes includ-ed dramatic arts, which taught poise and voice culture; home economics, where she continued her love of sewing beautiful clothes; archery; and her first love, literature and languages.

She and her classmates occasionally skipped church on Sundays to hang out at a popular restaurant, Jack Tray-er's Eat-In or Carry-Out in downtown Bristol. Sullins, like many women's colleges, had monthly dances when men from other schools were invited. The young men dressed in suits, and the young women wore party dresses. In the 1950s, all students were expected to be dressed in their best when attending dances and college games and going to town or chapel. Curfews were strict, as they were for me years later when I was at St. Mary's College. At St. Mary's, we had to be back on campus and signed in on weeknights by 10:30, if you even got permission to go out during the week. On weekends, curfews were 11:30. For Lind at Sullins the rules must have been similar.

Lind was on the president's council, part of the student government association composed of all the presidents and leaders of various organizations on campus. She auditioned for and was invited to join the school's singing group, the Cotton Pickers. The Cotton Pickers dressed in overalls, wore straw hats, dotted on eye-pencil freckles, and played ukuleles and bongos. Lind's instrument was castanets, or as a Cotton Picker would call them, clackers. The Pickers

The Cotton Pickers. Lind is left front.

played events at Sullins as well as in the community and at men's colleges nearby.

Before her first year at Sullins ended, Lind was named editor of *Reflector*, the Sullins College newspaper, for the coming 1956–57 school year. She was also third-floor monitor, the person responsible for checking on the other girls to be sure lights were out by eleven o'clock.

Lind was as respected and popular at Sullins College as she was at Boyden high school.

In the spring of her freshman year, Lind received an invitation to attend the Terpsichorean Club's thirtieth annual North Carolina Debutante Ball. It was to be held in the Raleigh Memorial Auditorium in September. She could invite one chief marshal and two assistant marshals.

Other invitations for parties soon followed from parents of debutantes throughout the state. Those parties would fill the summer before the ball. Lind asked Robert Wilson, Wyndham's friend from Charleston, to be her chief marshal, and though he said he was a bit surprised, he was flattered and accepted.

I will always be curious about her choosing Robert. Why not Jim, whom she dated all through high school? Perhaps she didn't know exactly when he would be returning from Germany. In addition, our parents were sure to have met Robert that previous summer when he and Lind had dated. They would have been impressed that he had gone to Episcopal High School in Virginia and was at Princeton, as well as being a friend of Wyndham's, whose parents they knew well. To Mom and Dad, he might have been a better choice. Whatever the reason, Robert was her chief marshal and not Jim.

Late in the spring of 1956, Jim did return home. Since neither Lind nor Jim had found anyone new they cared about, it was natural that they began dating again. Lind invited him to be one of her other marshals. Jim turned twenty-one in June and began working construction in Myrtle Beach, while staying in his parent's beach house. Lind must have visited him there.

Sometime in the middle or end of July, my sister realized she might be pregnant. She surely panicked. Having a baby out of wedlock in those days was not like it is today. There was a terrible stigma associated with it. In the 1950s, nice girls did not have sex—period. And they certainly did not get pregnant.

It is hard to exaggerate how horrifying this news would have been for her. Love and marriage, a working husband, the stay-at-home wife, the perfect children—that was what society expected. A whole family's reputation would be ruined forever if it was known a daughter even considered having sex before marriage. The South at that time could handle a murderer among its ranks with less public shame than an unwed mother.

Any woman caught in Lind's situation had few options. An abortion would have been illegal and, if discovered, a stain against the mother and her family that would be at least as great as that of the out-of-wedlock pregnancy itself.

Jim and Lind's high school relationship had lasted three years, a serious commitment for them. The music of the '50s was all about love, "Seventeen," "Fever," "Oh, What a Night," "Life Could Be a Dream," "Earth Angel," "Only Sixteen."

By the time they saw each other again in the summer of 1956, Jim had spent two maturing years in the army. Lind had lived away from home for a year, giving her a sense of freedom she'd not had before. When Jim came home, they were happy and excited to be together again. Since they could spend time alone in the beach cottage, it would have been hard for them to not "go all the way." Many couples did, but Lind was one of the unlucky ones. She got pregnant.

With the debutante ball in Raleigh fast approaching, Lind kept her worries a secret. Her first thoughts must have been how and when would she tell Mom and Dad. Certainly, not until after her debut. Mom, a Savannah debutante, was thrilled her daughter was invited to be one too. Lind couldn't take that away from her.

Maybe she wasn't really pregnant, just late. I would bet she was praying hard for some kind of miracle.

The deb ball in September came and went. By this time Lind must have known for sure she was pregnant. There is so much about my sister, her thoughts and emotions at that time and for years after, I will never know.

I do know our parents loved us, and that would have given Lind hope. Facing Mom would have been hard, but Mom was loving, easy, and empathetic. Facing Dad would be another thing. Lind and I were Daddy's special girls. We both worshiped him. He expected a lot of his three children. He was proud and strict—the typical '50s head of household— so normal for those times. In years to come, a pregnancy out of marriage might be a joyous and happy surprise, but in 1956 it was a disaster. Something I had never thought about until I learned more about my sister's experience.

The day Karen Garraputa from the Children's Home Society called me at my office, she sent me an email with a letter from Lind's son, John Davis, attached. The date was December 7, 2009. Karen wrote:

Hello Vaughan—One warning—you may not be any use at work the rest of the day. I understand that this process brings both joy and sorrow, as memories of the loss of this family connection and the grief your sister experienced, but may not have been able to express, are realized.

I have attached John's letter and some pictures. I know in exchange John would love to see a photo of his birth mother and his sister. I have also attached our reading list with suggestions. One book we recommend is The Girls Who Went Away *by Ann Fessler.*

I look forward to continuing to assist you in your reunion journey,
Karen

I immediately bought the book Karen suggested and read it cover to cover. It helped me immensely in understanding what my sister must have gone through. These young mothers suffered with insecurities, depression, illnesses, and occasionally committed suicide.

In the 1930s, '40s, and '50s when young women became pregnant out of wedlock, social workers encouraged them to give up their children to childless parents who "deserved them." Mothers could keep their babies if they wanted, but caseworkers pushed for only one choice: give up the baby for adoption. The pregnant mothers knew their children would be bastards if they didn't comply.

Was that the message my brilliant, beautiful sister was given? Did she live the rest of her life thinking of herself as undeserving?

My nephew John and I have discussed his birth and adoption many times since our first meeting in 2010. Together, we built a story around his conception and birth. We believed Lind and Jim had agreed to marry, have their baby, and maybe live with my parents until they could get on their feet. But, we told ourselves, Dad shut them down, refused to let them, and insisted Lind give the baby up for adoption.

Over the years, John had asked for any information the adoption agency was allowed to give him, but in our minds, it was never enough. Finally, in December of 2021 he petitioned post-adoption services again to see if there were any documents previously sealed that might be opened now.

We were both excited when they agreed to a Zoom call and promised to read to us all of the notes they had in their files about Lind and her pregnancy. John asked their permission to let us record the call, knowing we might not remember everything we heard. Afterwards, I had the recording transcribed so we could both have a copy.

From that Zoom call, we found out that the story we had put together was not the whole story. What we learned was definitely unexpected.

$$\sim 3 \sim$$

The following are excerpts from the transcript made from the Zoom call. The information we were given came from communications between the House of Mercy in Washington, DC, where Lind stayed until she had John, and the Children's Home Society in Greensboro, NC, where John would be sent to be adopted. Staff members from the House of Mercy made notes pertaining to Lind's time there. Mrs. Reed, a social worker employed by CHS, also kept records of her interactions with Lind.

> *On November 29, 1956, a Mrs. Guy who works at the House of Mercy informed the Children's Home Society [CHS] of Greensboro that Rosalind John-son Earle had been admitted to the House of Mercy the day before. That she was referred by Mr. Blair, rector of St. Luke's Episcopal Church in Salisbury, North Carolina. Lind expects to be delivering in March 1957. Mrs. Guy stated that Lind's parents would cover all costs for Lind's care; that Lind was interested in placing her child for adoption and*

would like Mrs. Reed, a Children's Home Society worker who lived in Washington to visit with her.

Mrs. Reed visited Lind throughout her stay at House of Mercy and communicated with CHS about how she was doing mentally and physically. Mrs. Reed also conducted an interview with our parents. Someone from CHS in Greensboro interviewed Jim, the birth father.

Mrs. Reed came to see Lind on November 30. She thought Lind looked very thin and frail. Her pregnancy didn't show at all. She made an appointment to return.

From an entry on December 27, 1956:

Lind and her parents came to Mrs. Reed's home in DC by appointment on December 27, 1956. Mrs. Reed secured all of the following information during a two-and-a half-hour interview.

Mrs. Reed's notes from the interview:

The baby's father, Jim, offered to marry Lind. He is much upset over the situation, feels that Lind is having to bear all the consequences of their act. Lind says she does not love him and feels it would be foolish to marry.

Lind is a very beautiful girl. She has gained weight and lost the gaunt, fragile look she had when worker first saw her [in November]. She has gray-blue eyes and beautifully shaped brows. Her hair is very dark brown, which she wears straight and brushed forward. Her skin is flawless. She is 5' 6"

*tall and weighs 110 pounds. Lind is a self-possessed
girl. Lind had told Mrs. Guy from the House of
Mercy she had a struggle facing the fact that she
was pregnant, but when she faced it and told her
parents, "she found peace."*

*The rector, Mr. Blair, has been most helpful to
Lind and her parents.*

No one is alive today who was in on those tough conversations. From the notes read to us on the Zoom call, I learned that Dad had called Thom Blair, our rector, for guidance. He counseled Dad that Lind should have the baby, but it would be wise of her to give it up for adoption. What a hard call that must have been for our father.

Lind then told Jim that he should go talk with Reverend Blair, and he did. He said he thought he would get a real scolding, but Reverend Blair was nice to him. Asked by Reverend Blair if he would marry Lind, Jim said certainly. But he felt at the time that all decisions were made by our dad. He confessed he was not assertive in making any of those decisions. He was not allowed to see or speak with Lind. And he never did again that he can remember.

Hearing that makes me sad. I can't even imagine how he was feeling. This baby would be his child as well as hers. He had been in Lind's life since she was a freshman in high school.

The interview at Mrs. Reed's house continues:

*Lind's mother says Lind sings very well. She makes
good grades in school and in college and is very
active in school activities.*

Lind has never had but two boyfriends during high school. She went steady with Jim Rabon (the baby's father). Parents said they never knew Jim very well as he is a very quiet boy.

Last summer [the summer of 1956] Lind met a young man while she was visiting her grand-mother in Savannah, Georgia. She was apparently much attracted to this young man, age 21. He is a Princeton graduate from an excellent family. He is presently a second-year medical student at the University of Virginia. He came to visit Lind at Sullins about Thanksgiving time. She told him of her pregnancy.

She expected this to be the end of their relation-ship. On the contrary, after a night of soul-search-ing this young man returned and insisted that she accompany him to her parent's home in Salisbury and tell them what had occurred. He took her to Salisbury personally. He has been most understand-ing and helpful. He has visited her since she came to Washington.

It seems that his support has been the deciding factor in enabling her to accept her pregnancy. He is decidedly favorable to having the child surrendered for adoption.

What? Lind met and was dating someone other than Jim? It wasn't Robert Wilson, Wyndham's friend, who she dated the summer before in Charleston. It was someone else—a medical student she met in Savannah when we were all visiting our grandparents the previous June, some-one neither John nor I knew existed.

I had no inkling there was anyone else in Lind's life. I could understand falling for a new man while not knowing she was pregnant. After all, she was only nineteen years old. But if she continued dating someone she met in Savannah knowing she was pregnant, she must have really fallen for him. Neither John nor I knew what to say to that. We felt protective of John's father, Jim, and we were attached to our version of events. Our silence on hearing this must have been palpable. We were stunned.

I asked if there was a name mentioned for this other boyfriend. The person from CHS on Zoom said there wasn't, she had read the notes before and would have remembered a name. I couldn't believe his name was not mentioned in the notes. Who was this guy?

Mrs. Reed's notes continue:

Lind's parents are both rather good-looking. Mr. Earle is rather handsome. He is forty-five and the owner of an office supply store. He was born in Virginia but came to Salisbury as a young boy and returned later after marrying and having two children. He graduated from NC State College. He is a leader in the church and civic affairs in Salisbury. He served in World War II, mostly in the Pacific.

Lind's mother is rather pretty, though her features are not as good as her daughter's. She does not have Lind's style. She was reared in Savannah, Georgia. Mrs. Earle studied music and attended Brenau Conservatory. She plays the piano and is interested in music. She is a Girl Scout leader and is also active in St. Luke's Episcopal Church.

*Lind's mother said Lind's pregnancy was the
most unexpected blow she had ever had. She is
totally unable to understand the attitude of Lind's
generation about sex. She feels in some way that she
and Lind's father have failed. Lind assured them in
the worker's presence that they had not failed, but
that she, Lind, had failed.*

*Mrs. Earle said that she wanted it to be in the
record that Lind's father has "the best disposition
in the world." And that he seems to be making the
most of a difficult situation. Her chief problem now
was parrying questions about Lind's absence from
home from relatives, friends, and neighbors. They
have told relatives and friends that Lind was run
down and had tuberculosis in an early stage.*

*Mr. Earle says he tells people he was able to get
Lind medical care as a veteran dependent in Washington. So that is where they sent her for treatment.*

Lying was just not in my parent's wheelhouse, and doing
so must have been so difficult for them. But to say their
unmarried daughter was pregnant would have been much
worse.

Mrs. Reed's notes indicate she suggested that Mrs. Earle
not try to explain Lind's absence unless she is forced to answer direct questions. To say as little as possible, just that
her health is improving, and she will soon be able to return
home.

*All four of Lind's grandparents are living and in
good health. Her seventy-six-year-old paternal
grandmother [Bam] still plays golf. The paternal
grandfather [Pop], seventy-one, is retired and is in*

good health. Lind's maternal grandfather [Blake], eighty-two, walks every day. His hobby is growing camellias. The maternal grandmother [Bessie Kate], sixty-three, loves to fish and crab and is a wonderful southern cook. There is no evidence of prolonged illness or any medical problems on either side of the family that worker was able to discover.

Lind's brother, Gordon Merrick Earle, Jr., is age sixteen. He is a very good-looking boy. He is about six feet tall and 165 pounds. He has blue eyes and brown hair. He is in the eleventh grade.

The youngest child, Harriet Vaughan, is seven years old. She is an exceptionally fine-looking little girl with gray-blue eyes and blonde hair, which is rapidly turning dark.

When my parents went for the interview with the House of Mercy in December 1956, they must have taken photos of Rick and me with them.

After I learned about Lind's pregnancy in 2009, I asked my brother if he had known. He said our parents told him Lind was sick and was sent away to recover. He thought no more about it.

I don't remember them telling me anything. I probably thought she had gone back to college.

Lind's health has been good, and she has had all of her shots. She did have a tonsillectomy as a little girl but had forgotten it until her parents mentioned it.

Lind and her parents discussed with Mrs. Reed the process of surrendering the infant and transporting the baby to CHS in Greensboro. [Lind's] parents do not want to see the baby.

[Mrs. Reed] *asked about the birth father. They said he is very handsome. He is "picture-book pretty." According to Mr. Earle, he is an excellent athlete. He is now a freshman at Catawba College in Salisbury. He is not an intellectual giant but does get along fine scholastically.*

Jim's family is not of the same social stratum as the Earle family. His grandmother operates a small bakery and the family lives over the shop. His father drives a truck. Jim will doubtless visit Greensboro and CHS for an interview. Lind stated several times that this baby would be very beautiful.

From Mrs. Reed's next visit, January 18, 1957:

Visited Lind at House of Mercy on several occasions since last dictation. When I saw her during the past week or so, she has not looked so well. She seemed pale and her attitude is different. She was very brusque with me on one occasion, saying that she has been roused from a nap, and it was around eleven a.m. However, when I saw her on January 17 and told her that Jim had made an appointment to visit Greensboro, she was more vivacious and thanked me.

CHS notes on January 23, 1957:

Mr. Jim Rabon came to CHS in Greensboro for his interview. He seems a robust and healthy young man. I suppose he could be termed handsome. He was a little shy and withdrawn at first and never did really loosen up during the interview to talk spontaneously.

Though he only answered direct questions, she didn't feel he was holding anything back. It seemed hard for Mr. Rabon to make it clear to her that adoption was not his idea, but Lind's. He still want- ed to marry Lind, and I thought he was quite hurt by her rejection.

He filled out the family history form. Mr. Ra- bon's jaw was hurt while playing football in Germa- ny, and he does not talk distinctly. I certainly felt from my talk with this young man and from what he told me about his family history, that this baby would have a sound, healthy heredity.

I learned from John that Jim decided he would never tell his mother. And why would he? The relationship with Lind was over. Everything was decided for him, and he couldn't change it. I personally believe Jim is a very kind and caring man who must have carried scars from this the rest of his life—just as I believe my sister did.

Mrs. Reed writes:

Lind is not relating well to the other girls in the home. She is inclined to be snobbish. Mrs. Guy plans to talk this out with Lind and will discuss the matter with me later.

Mrs. Reed's notes on January 26,1957:

Lind's friend is coming to see her. She has permis- sion to be out until nine p.m. on Saturday and may spend Sunday afternoon with him. She looked well and seemed very happy about seeing her friend. She

*gave me her birth certificate as well as the mid-se-
mester grades she made at Sullins. Her grades were
one A plus, two A's, a B, and a C.*

Mrs. Reed's visit on March 4, 1957:

*It was a beautiful day, so we went for a ride. [Lind]
seems well physically. Mrs. Guy told me that the
young man who attends medical college is having
a difficult time. His relatives have found out about
Lind's pregnancy and are very much disturbed
about his association with her. Lind has informed
him that he is released from any obligation towards
her. However, the young man is very loyal to her.*

Mrs. Reed's visit on March 16, 1957:

*She seems happy and at peace. Her friend from
UVA plans to drive her back to Salisbury in his car
as soon as she is discharged from House of Mercy.*

Mrs. Reed's note on March 22, 1957:

*Lind has her baby. She named him James Carlton
Earle.*

Mrs. Reed's note on March 30, 1957:

Lind signs surrender papers on this date.

Note written by a House of Mercy staff member on
March 31, 1957:

*The baby is flown from DC to Greensboro by Mrs.
Reed and admitted to the nursery.*

April 5, 1957:

*Lind plans to leave the House of Mercy and return
to her home. She will write to Mrs. Reed in about
two weeks.*

I am not sure if Lind and the UVA medical student ever
saw each other again. He probably obeyed his parents' wish-
es to break it off with her. I just wonder what might have
happened with the relationship if she had not been pregnant. Would they have continued dating, gotten married?
It haunts me, wondering how different her life might have
been. Did she ever think about that too? She must have.

The CHS records included a note Lind wrote a month
after her baby's birth. The letter, dated April 24, 1957, was
sent from Salisbury.

Dear Mrs. Reed,

*Our month is about up now, and I am awfully
anxious to hear that my son is happily placed with
his loving parents. I haven't changed my mind at
all. My concern is for his happiness.*

*It's been so grand being with my family. No
home could have opened its arms wider to a prod-
igal daughter. I've seen many friends who have all
been thoughtful and kind—no unpleasant encoun-
ters at all.*

*My plans are complete now for college, beginning
this summer. I'm quite ready to start back to work.*

Again, Mrs. Reed, I want to thank you for your many kindnesses.

Give [name redacted] a big hug and kiss for me when next you're in Greensboro.

Many thanks and my sincere love.

Lind

From Mrs. Reed's notes, May 6, 1957:

Baby "Devon" as he was known at the Children's Home Society was placed in the home of Reverend and Mrs. John Davis of Rocky Mount.

While Lind had been going through her pregnancy at the House of Mercy, CHS had been looking through applications from couples who wanted to adopt. One family stood out. Several years before, they had adopted a baby girl and let CHS know they would love to have another child. They fit all the criteria that Lind and our parents had asked for. They were exceptional people and would give this child a loving home.

$$\sim 4 \sim$$

After the shock of hearing about the other man Lind was dating, I was desperate to learn the identity of this thoughtful person who stood by Lind's side throughout her stressful, anxious, and most likely, lonely time at House of Mercy. I wondered if he might be the third man in the debutante photo. The timing was certainly right for him to be one of her marshals.

I asked the post-adoption services representative again if she was sure his name was not anywhere in the records; she assured me that it wasn't.

I emailed the debutante photo to Wyndham—Lind's high school friend who had been a debutante the same year—she pointed out Jim Rabon and her friend Robert Wilson but did not know who the other marshal was. She suggested I contact Robert, that he might remember his name.

Thoughts about this Savannah boyfriend I never knew existed wouldn't leave me alone.

When I was growing up our family would always visit Mom's parents in Savannah, usually sometime early in the summer. My grandmother, Kathryn would take me crabbing at Tybee Island. Rick and Dad would help granddad

Blake with any repairs the house needed. And Lind would be set up on dates, as I was when I was older. If this mystery man was one of them, I must have met him then too, but I don't remember him at all.

I do, however, have a vivid memory of a guy coming from out of town to visit Lind one summer. Maybe it was that debutante summer. It might or might not be a memory of the Savannah guy, but I would like to believe it was.

I had heard her talk about him to our parents. She warned me to behave and not to talk too much. By the time he showed up at our house, I was almost as excited as Lind. I knew they would go off in his car and not stay at the house long.

When he rang the doorbell, I ran to open it, and what Lind had said was right. He was so good-looking, tall, dark, with beautiful eyes, a great smile, and he was nice to me. I wanted to show him just how wonderful I thought he was, so while he and Lind were talking with Mom and Dad, I sneaked outside and taped wrapped chewing gum, my poetry, artwork, and daisies from our yard all over his car.

When they came out, my sister was upset, which embarrassed me. But he said it was fine and he loved it. That made me love him too. I was seven.

I must have heard his name at the time, but over the years, I had forgotten it. Yet there was a name stuck in my head forever, a name belonging to a good-looking man I had met somewhere—and that name was Julian. Was Julian the UVA student she had met in Savannah and the handsome man that came to visit and was so nice to me?

I sent the information I had been given on the CHS Zoom call to Robert Wilson. He texted that he might know who the mystery man was. Robert then sent me a photo of a student he had known at Episcopal High School. He was the right age. He had gone to Princeton and UVA medical school and was from Savannah. His name was Julian Kelly. Julian. The name I remembered my whole life. I had goose-bumps when I read Robert's text and saw the photo. Julian. Handsome. Dark hair, dark eyes, great smile.

The person Robert identified had died in February of 2021. I was so disappointed and sad that I missed talking with him and learning the absolute truth of his relationship with my sister by only one year.

Robert sent me a link to his obituary.

> [Julian] *was a lifetime member of Christ Episcopal Church. He remarked often that one of the things he admired most about his father was how kind he was to everyone he met, a trait that Julian also practiced throughout his lifetime. He was a consummate gentleman.*

I was sure Robert had found the right person.

I texted Robert back and asked if Julian was the mystery man in the debutante photo I had sent him. Robert said he didn't think so. He said if Julian had been the third marshal, he would know it because he had known Julian from school. Could I trust Robert's memory? I wanted that third marshal to be the Julian I remembered and the man who was so kind to Lind. Now it was up to me to keep on digging.

Soon after hearing from Robert, I went to the Rowan Public Library in Salisbury to search through the microfilm of newspapers from 1956 and found the announcement of the debutantes and their marshals. There it was.

Lind's escorts were Robert Wilson of Charleston, S.C. as her chief marshal and two marshals—James Rabon of Salisbury and Julian Kelly of Savannah.

The Julian from my subconscious. He must have made
a huge impression on me as well as on Lind.

A question I ask myself is why. Why had I not wondered
earlier who the marshals in the deb photo were? Why had
I not thought it was important until I found out there had
been another man Lind was dating while pregnant? So many
whys. Such a big regret. If I had found the article in the paper
earlier I might have talked with Julian. It seems it was not
meant to be.

Jim Rabon, Robert Wilson, Lind, and Julian Kelly

— 5 —

Shortly after John and I began emailing in 2010, he sent me the information his adoptive parents received when they were considering adopting him as their son. The following is typical of the information available to adopting parents at the time.

This is an excerpt from the Children's Home Society's non-identifying records:

> The baby was born on March 22, 1957, in Washington, DC, at 5:22 p.m. It was a full-term pregnancy. He weighed 7 pounds, 5 ounces and was 20 inches long. He was described as a long baby with blue eyes, healthy, normal.
>
> The birth mother was 19 years of age. The birth mother planned to continue her education. She enjoyed literature, drama, fashion, and writing. She was described as beautiful. The birth mother's father owned a business and was a college graduate. The birth mother's mother had completed one year of study at a music conservatory. The birth mother's parents were both 45.

The nationality descent of the birth mother's family was English on her maternal side and Scottish on her paternal side.

The religious affiliation for the birth mother was Episcopalian.

The birth father was 21 years of age. He had graduated high school and was a sophomore in college. He lived with his family. He served two years in the army. He was described as an excellent athlete. He was a full-time student and worked construction during school holidays. The birth father was described as quiet at first meeting.

The birth father's father was 43 years of age and graduated high school. He was employed as a sales route manager. He enjoyed gardening. The birth father's mother was age 44 and graduated high school. She was employed as a department store clerk. The birth father was an only child. A grandmother operated a bakery. The grandfather was a business owner.

The birth father injured his jaw while playing football in the service and this left him with a little speech defect. His paternal grandfather was living and in good health.

Both maternal grandparents died when he was an infant.

The nationality descent of the birth father's family was German on his maternal side and Scotch-Irish on his paternal side.

The religious affiliation for the birth father was Methodist.

The birth mother was very concerned that a loving plan be made for the baby. She wanted the baby

to have the advantages and opportunities that two
parents could provide. She thought carefully about
her decision and demonstrated maturity. She want-
ed the baby to have a college education and a family
with close relationships, love, and respect. The birth
father assisted in planning for adoption.

Interesting that they would write that. The birth father
didn't assist—he couldn't assist. Even if Jim had wanted to
adopt his son, he was not allowed.

John also sent me information about his adoptive parents. It made me feel good when I read about them. Lind
and our parents would have been pleased with the Home
Society's choice too, I am sure.

The Reverend John (Johnny) William Sutphin
Davis was born in Henderson, North Carolina, on
June 17, 1923. He attended Episcopal High School
in Alexandria, Virginia, and graduated from the
University of North Carolina at Chapel Hill. John-
ny served as a naval flight instructor in World War
II. After the war, he attended Virginia Theological
Seminary and was ordained with the Episcopal
Diocese of North Carolina.

Sarah Davis was born in Cramerton, North
Carolina, in 1924. She graduated from the Nation-
al Cathedral School in Washington, DC, and from
St. Mary's College in Raleigh, as well as Women's
College of the University of North Carolina [now
UNC-Greensboro].

Johnny and Sarah had already adopted a daughter, who was four years old when James joined their family. They renamed their adopted son John William, Jr.

In 1957, the year Johnny and Sarah adopted John, three Durham families took steps toward establishing a new church. With the support of the vestry at St. Philip's Church in downtown Durham, St. Stephen's Episcopal Church became a reality, and Reverend John Davis became its first rector. Frank Kenan was elected senior warden. Frank and his wife Betty Kenan became great supporters of the church and good friends with Johnny and Sarah. John's godparents were Melville Broughton, the son of a North Carolina governor, and his wife, who was a close friend of Sarah's. Other godparents were June Bourne Long and Reverend Tom Smyth, who attended Virginia Theological Seminary with Johnny.

John was adopted by loving parents who also knew and moved among some of the most successful people in North Carolina. They provided him with a strong and secure upbringing. But when John found out he was adopted, he could not help but wonder about the family he did not know.

— 6 —

Lind must have had a hard time when she returned home to Salisbury to spend that spring with our parents. Despite what Lind said in the letter to Mrs. Reed, she knew she had been marked as "promiscuous." Her friends were "thoughtful and kind." They were surely questioning what had gone on with her. Did she really have TB or was that a cover up? If she had been pregnant, why didn't Jim ask her to marry him? Or if he did, did she turn him down? They had been a couple for so long. What had happened?

Maybe a few friends knew the truth, but I am sure my parents had told her to never talk about it with anyone.

Lind was probably ready to leave home as soon as possible. She enrolled in UNC-Chapel Hill in May 1957 and declared her major in classics.

Later, as I was going off to college at St. Mary's in Raleigh, Mom told me Lind had confessed that a few times her first year at Chapel Hill she awoke in the morning on a strange front lawn after drinking the night before. She began smoking then too. When Mom mentioned this to me, I thought she meant I should be careful about drinking and smoking. But now I would guess Lind was drinking and smoking because she was racked with guilt over giving up her baby just three months before and hurting Jim, whom she had once cared so much about, and was sad about losing the young man from Savannah. All of that was in addition to the shame she felt having done this to our parents.

Yet Lind seemed determined to turn her life around. She was smart, loved learning, and happy to be out of Salisbury and at the university. She could now be distracted by her studies and by making new friends who had no knowledge of her past.

But like practically every other twenty-year-old woman in the late 1950s, she might have felt some desperation to marry—to make amends in a way. My sister seemed to attract men easily. The next year she dodged at least one bullet in that department.

Sometime in the spring or summer of 1958, Lind became engaged. I was nine years old at the time, so I don't remember much about him, but I do recall the dramatic, tearful end to the relationship. We'd gone to my parents' cabin on High Rock Lake just outside of Salisbury. After dinner, my sister and her fiancé walked down to the dock while Mom, Dad, and I sat on the deck above. We couldn't see them in the semi-darkness, but we could hear them, and what we heard turned ugly.

"You've been keeping it from me," Lind shouted. "I should have known. I certainly saw how you behaved at dinner tonight—in front of my parents. You just couldn't get enough drinks in you. You were embarrassing." Her voice became shrill.

"I'm so sorry. It won't happen again," he pleaded. "I promise, Lind. I really love you."

Mom and Dad quickly ushered me inside, and not long after, Lind rushed through the door, obviously very upset. She burst out crying. "I threw my engagement ring into the lake, and, oh my god, it was his grandmother's ring," she sobbed. "But I was so angry."

Her now ex-fiancé did not follow after her, and, moments later, we heard him screech away, tearing down our gravel road in his car.

Lind was shaking and trying to calm herself.

"I hadn't seen him drunk like this before. A friend warned me he had a serious drinking problem and, boy, were they right.

"He got himself into some trouble in the past, evidently. When I asked him about it, he said he had kicked it and he was fine. But he didn't seem fine tonight, did he? I'm so sorry, Mom and Dad."

She went on, listing the reasons she broke up with him. She said he confessed to her that alcoholism runs in his family. He promised he would stop right then—for good—for her—if she would just marry him. He loved her.

She continued, trying to make sense of it all to our parents. Was this another shameful thing she had done to them? She had to explain that she didn't know.

"I feel awful about his grandmother's ring, but I was so upset. I can't believe the mess I almost got myself into. I could have been killed in a car wreck. He could have killed us both, or someone else. You heard him leave here." Lind paused to get her breath. "Marrying him would have been a disaster."

I don't know if Lind carried this scar with her, too, but it surely must have affected the way she felt about herself.

Luckily, things took a more positive turn over the next few years.

During the summer of 1959, Lind stayed in Atlanta with Penelope Brown Barnett, a close cousin of Mom's, and Penelope's husband, Crawford. She had snagged a coveted job at Rich's Department Store on its College Board, advising college-bound women about their wardrobes.

That summer, Lind was also in the August 1959 college issue of *Mademoiselle,* in an article titled "Modeling Collector's Shirts." She was the only model with a pixie haircut; Lind was always ahead of fashion trends.

～ 7 ～

September 1959, back in Chapel Hill, Lind rented a one-bedroom house on Clark Court and found a small group of intelligent, creative, and fun-loving men whom she would stay in close contact with for the rest of her life.

Scott Griffith, an English major who would become one of those lifelong friends, wrote me an email about meeting my sister.

> Your sister had, among much else, a rebellious streak, I would say. It may be that quality which first attracted me to her. I had been sent to her by a mutual friend who suggested she might be able to help me out of a hole I was in concerning a girl we both knew. I rang Lind's bell, introduced myself, and explained my difficulty. We exchanged personal details—although I was an undergraduate, I was still slightly older than Lind because I'd done my military service before college—and she agreed to help if she could. She did.
>
> But in the meantime, I'd got the agreeable sense that, beneath appearances, she could be much

more than the conventional Carolina student—an intellectual, more prepared to entertain ideas, to use honest language, to laugh at social absurdities, accepting of things which appalled or shocked or frightened many girls her age in the late fifties. That's the kind of rebelliousness I have in mind.

In 1960, a memory I have that illustrates the winning insouciance Lind could display concerns a summer term adventure some of us cooked up at Chapel Hill. We got together some spare lumber and empty oil drums and concocted a raft and proposed to float down the river—which one I don't recall. Each of us invited a girl along so that the raft numbered, maybe eight of us. I invited Lind.

Somehow, with the aid of someone's car and a trailer we got our raft to the waterside and set off. There was good food; plenty of beer; song singing; and talk that, as the hours wore on, became less and less animated—the day being hot, even on the shaded murky river. We looked at the water, the color of Coca-Cola and wondered what was beneath the surface, whether there were snakes and snapping turtles.

After a while, Lind, when the lack of action must have seemed to her interminable, abruptly stood, stripped down to a slip she had on, and dived right in. Plop! She came back up to the surface, unscratched, and within seconds all the rest, though maybe not all the girls, were in the water too, hooting and splashing and having a fine time, refreshed and happy, and all thanks to Lind's courageous/exasperated/rebellious example.

Years later, speaking to [our friends] Frank Nye and Norton Tennille about other things, I declared

*that I had been a genuine rebel in those days—still
was. Frank said no. Lind was the biggest rebel of
all, and I, thinking of that raft trip, had to see the
truth in what he said.*

I love this reminiscence about Lind. Seeing her through
Scott's eyes shows me that my sister was not a shrinking
violet. She had been through so much. It is good to realize
she never lost her strong will and spirit of fun. I am finding out she was braver and bolder than I have ever been. I
would have been just like the rest of them—holding back.

My sister dressed impeccably and purchased interesting
objects thoughtfully, just as the handwriting analysis had
suggested. In 1960, Lind saw a carving of a Japanese figure
in Paces Gift Shop in Chapel Hill's Glen Lennox Shopping Center. When she went back to buy it, it was gone.
She asked the owner of the shop if it had been sold. She
was told the buyer was Max Steele, an English teacher at
UNC, and he had taken it with him to New Orleans. Lind
begged for his address and wrote to him about buying the
Japanese figure.

Max wrote her back and told her he would sell it to her
for seventy-five dollars and he would pay postage or sev-
enty dollars and he would send it collect. Lind wrote him
back asking if she could break up the payments and send
him twenty-five dollars a month for three months. He generously agreed. Max and Lind wrote back and forth until
the final payment, when she sent more than he asked for.

10 April 1961

Dear Lind—

I knew you had paid much too much but wasn't sure how much too much. But thanks for your neat letter—and for wanting to pay more than the set-price.

Herewith my check for $5.00 in partial repayment. Please cash it because it is already deducted from my account.

In further repayment, I'll send you, when my trunks arrive from New Orleans, some pre-Columbian Aztec clay fragments. They're small and not important but they are authentic (from John Huston's collection, which he began while making The Treasure of the Sierra Madre) and I think you may like them.

Thanks again for your generosity and thoughtfulness.

Best, Max

After my sister's graduation from UNC-Chapel Hill in 1962, she found a job as a layout editor for a farm journal in Hillsborough, North Carolina. She continued to live in the small rental on Clark Court in Chapel Hill. Norton Tennille, another classics major and Lind's close college friend, wrote me about their time together then.

As I recall, it was a somewhat down-at-the heels clapboard house of the type seen throughout rural North Carolina. There, the similarity with such houses ended. It was a magical place to me because

*it was full of books and records! There weren't that
many southern girls who would have collected them,
certainly not the ones I knew. Somehow, it was
like stepping out of a Chapel Hill dominated (for
me) by fraternity boys and sorority girls and into a
Narnian wardrobe. I saw a whole new world—one
I liked very much and have tried to remain in since
that time.*

Norton also included a poem by Dawn Potter, a Maine
poet. A poet himself, Norton found Potter's poem evoca-
tive of his time in Chapel Hill and the good times he spent
with Lind and their friends, Scott Griffith and Frank Nye:

Nostalgia
It was darker then, in the nights when the cars
Came sliding around the traffic circle, when the
    headlights
Speckled with rain traveled the bedroom walls,
and vanished; when the typewriter, the squeaking
    chair,
the slow voice of the radio stirred the night air like a
    fan.
Of course, the ones we loved were beautiful—
slim, dark-haired, intent on their books.
The rain came swishing against the lamp-lit windows.
The cat purred in his chair. A clock sang,
and we lay nearly asleep, almost dreaming,
almost alone, nearly gone—the days fly so;
and the nights, like sleep, disappear without memory.

Norton comments:

What does the poem say? The nights were darker then. Especially in small towns like Chapel Hill. Fewer, less powerful streetlights, I suppose. And because darker, also softer—you could actually hear the rain. There were no air conditioners. The windows had screens and would be open, letting in the breeze and such noise as there might be.

Headlights swept through the bedroom at night, and if it was raining, the beams were speckled with rain. A car turning a corner, or just passing by, created the same effect. We had typewriters and squeaky chairs, and yes, "the slow voice of the radio stirred the night air like a fan."

Imagine Lind living in that one-bedroom house, in bed listening to a radio and the rain. For all of Lind's infectious laughter, and a smile that was warm and flattering and even a bit seductive, she was a deeply reflective and often sad person. Perhaps melancholy is too strong a word, but it was clear that she suffered; it was not something she ever shared with me, but it was apparent from her moods.

Lind was "beautiful, slim, dark-haired, and intent on her books." And we all loved her for it. She was too thin, I think, probably because she smoked so much.

I imagine Lind lying alone in that house late at night "almost dreaming, nearly gone."

Which brings us back to the reality of Frank, Scott, and I, her friends, "the days fly so; and the nights, like sleep, disappear without memory."

When I read the poem and Norton's reminiscence, I felt sadness, a sense of loss for them and for me. I was too young to know my sister well during those years, and their close friendship sounded so romantic. I regret not being one of them, a part of their lives.

Lind did let me visit one weekend when I was eleven. My parents put me on the bus in Salisbury, and I rode to Chapel Hill by myself. How I loved Lind's little house, just one main room, a bedroom the size of the bed, and a tiny bath. Lind had built a long bookshelf with concrete blocks and wooden boards to separate her living room from her tiny kitchen. Her sofa served as my bed. My sister loved all kinds of music and had hundreds of records, which she played night and day. That weekend, the music flowed, along with conversation, smoking, laughter, and Frank Nye.

Frank had dark brown hair and deep blue eyes. He was in Chapel Hill pursuing his master's and PhD in English. Though he and my sister talked about many things I could not grasp, Frank always, in some way, tried to include me. He writes:

> I was living in a house in Carrboro, a town adjacent to Chapel Hill, with two roommates. We gave a party, and Scott was invited. He brought Lind as his date. At least that's the way I remember our meeting. At any rate, I remember that Lind and I got along very well from the first, based largely, I believe, on our mutual interests in classical music (especially opera) and books. I'm not sure how she knew Scott and Norton. She had recently received her BA in classics from UNC, and since Norton was also a classics major, they may have met in class.

Lind and I spent many hours together listening to music and talking. I remember that her favorite operatic composer was Wagner, and she was also fond of the symphonies of Sibelius. One of her favorite authors was Graham Greene.

In any case, the three of us became fast friends, and we met at her little rented one-bedroom house at 5 Clark Court in Chapel Hill regularly in the afternoons that summer, after she'd get off work, when the three of us would drive out to Hogan's Lake to take a swim.

I had known that Lind had had a child previous to my knowing her, from early on in our friendship, because I had been told about it by two acquaintances (who didn't know each other, I think) from Salisbury. One was a fraternity brother of mine at Davidson, and the other was a student at UNC who had dated a girl I knew at Queens College. But Lind never told me.

She was a warm and kind person, very intelligent, very much a lady when circumstances called for her to be, and at times she was delightfully outspoken. I'll never forget the time that my mother was visiting me in Chapel Hill, and we got together with Lind. Lind was describing to my mother the swimming trips we'd taken to Hogan's Lake. There was a sort of dilapidated water ski jump in the middle of the lake, and Lind told my mother that one time we swam out to the ski jump and there was a turd sitting in the middle of it. I'd never have dared use that word in front of my mother, but to my relief my mother laughed. My mother liked Lind.

Frank had been an undergraduate at Davidson College and spent a year in Paris studying at the Sorbonne. He had just returned to Chapel Hill in the fall of 1962, when he met Lind. From Frank's email I learned more about the music she loved and an author she liked. So I listened to Sibelius's symphonies and read Graham Greene just to be a bit closer to understanding her. And as for Frank's story about what they found on the ski jump, I easily agreed that the Lind who was completely unworried about stating facts, regardless of who she was speaking to, was the sister I came to know when I was older.

Frank loved all the things Lind loved—opera, poetry, reading the classics, and philosophical discussions lasting long into the night. Though absolutely the perfect man for my sister, he never told her—and, apparently, she never guessed—he was gay.

Clark Court rental house where Lind lived for several years.

— 8 —

The day I received that call from the Children's Home Society, I could think of nothing except Lind's son. I had no idea where he was, but he wanted to meet us. I could have lived my entire life never knowing he existed. I went home early. Don had gone out.

When I heard Don drive up, I hurried to the door. "I want to hear every word of that phone call from CHS."

"Actually, I thought it was a call from the Carolina Alumni Association. She didn't really identify herself well, or maybe I was distracted. The woman gave her name and said she was trying to find Lind Earle. I said she'd been living in Paris, but sadly, she had died. I also gave her your work number and said you were her sister. She thanked me and hung up. That was it."

In 1963, Lind was twenty-six and decided to travel abroad. I was a freshman at Boyden High School. Rick had graduated in industrial engineering from NC State, served in the army, and was planning to go back to work at Buffalo Forge in Buffalo, New York, as soon as he got out.

Rick recalls Lind working hard and saving money so she could travel to Austria for the Salzburg Music Festival. That was a dream of hers, he said. Afterwards, she took a train to Paris to visit with Frank's friend, Brigitte Buire. Once in Paris, she decided to stay, at least for a while.

Ever since I visited Lind in Chapel Hill and met Frank, I thought they would make a perfect couple. Later, when she left, I wondered if she had run away to France because he never asked her to marry him.

Frank believed he couldn't share with Lind his sexual orientation:

It's hard today for people to realize how difficult it was back then to be openly gay, even with friends. But I'm still amazed that she didn't know. Most of my straight friends knew, and there was no need to talk about it. I think that homosexuality just wasn't on her radar. Most importantly, I was very afraid that, if I told her, she would no longer be interested in being a friend of mine, and she was too dear to me to take that risk. And, to tell you the truth, I'm still not sure she could have handled the news. Complicating matters, if I had my secret that I'd never shared with her, she had a secret she'd never shared with me.

Whatever the reasons, getting away seemed right for Lind. She could leave her disappointments behind and create a new and exciting life. It may also have been important for her to put some serious distance between her secret and anyone who might know about it. But I also believe my sister thrived on the challenges of a new language and different culture. Frank certainly thought so:

This was typical of her. She was independent and unafraid of putting herself in a place where she didn't speak the language and where she knew no one. I encouraged her to do it, because I was afraid she was getting too attached to me, and because I thought it would be good for her to be in a new and exciting place. I had made friends there I knew she'd like.

When Lind moved to Paris, I got in touch with my old friends—among them Francois Capber, Brigitte Buire, and Henri Behar—and they welcomed her into their lives, found her a place to live, and even a job teaching English. She had a real gift for languages. Within three months, she was writing me letters in French, and quickly her French got better and better until it was fluent.

Brigitte Buire, who had grown up in Paris, and Lind hit it off so well, they decided to room together. They shared a large four-bedroom apartment on the Rue de Rome facing the below-the-surface railroad tracks leading to the Gare St-Lazare. The apartment they rented was owned by the parents of another friend of Frank's, Jacques Passelac.

Brigitte wrote me in the spring of 2020:

I have been trying to remember details about my life with Lind then. Unfortunately, my memory is failing me these days. All the more so as this was a very difficult and painful period of my life. My mother, who was divorcing my father, had kicked me out of the house—the reason why I ended up living with Lind.

We led a very pleasant life, and the apartment was always full of friends, especially on the

*weekends. At the time I was writing my thesis, and
Lind would help me correct my English and would
type a few pages for me. She was much quicker than
me with the typewriter!*

*What I remember very well is that she would
amble around the house all day long holding her
eternal cup of tea, under which she would put a
kitchen napkin—rather a tissue—at the time. Since
then I have done the same thing with my daily cup
of tea at four o'clock!*

*As I mentioned, my memory is not too good
these days, though I try to exercise it every day by
reading in four different languages! Your sister was
quite secretive and had never even hinted at what
had happened to her in her youth.*

*Her life must have been indeed sad; she had the
burden of her abandoned child to carry, but she was
not a sad person. She was lively and could prove
enthusiastic—especially (later on) when she went to
Austria to listen to operas with her Austrian friend,
Tatyana, for example.*

In the summer of 1965, Frank flew to France and joined
Lind and Jacques on a trip to the Loire Valley to see various
châteaux. Frank then stayed with Lind and Brigitte. Frank's
ex-lover, Francois, who was in the army, came on weekend
leave to spend time with the three of them. Frank told me
about his earlier relationship with Francois.

*I met Francois in Paris on Halloween night, 1962,
and we quickly became lovers. We never actually
lived together, but we spent six of every seven nights*

together, and I was always invited to his mother's home for lunch on Sundays. Our relationship was always veering from being very loving and affectionate to his retreating from it because of terrible guilt for being gay. About once a month, he'd tell me that he couldn't see me anymore, and we'd break up. Then he'd see a Catholic priest or a psychologist, they'd tell him it was okay, and he'd beg me to come back to him. I always did, but it wore me out, because it kept happening and never seemed to get better.

While Frank and Francois were there with Brigitte and Lind, Frank witnessed a relationship develop quickly between Francois and Lind.

He popped in bed with Lind, with me sleeping in the next room. I am sure Brigitte had told Lind about my sexuality by that time. I have thought about what was going on many, many times, and I'll never know for sure, but I suspect this was an attempt on Francois's part to get even with me for rejecting him. Maybe something of the same sort was going on with Lind. On the other hand, both of them were very attractive people, and Francois was bisexual, so maybe they'd been attracted to each other since she'd arrived in Paris. Francois came down on leave on the weekends, and he and Lind always slept together when he was there.

Not long after, another friend of Frank's, Gerard Reddon, invited Frank and Lind to his family's house on the French Riviera for a house party.

Lind at a house party on the French Riviera.

Following the party, Frank and Lind took the train to Venice. On the way, Lind confided that Francois had asked her to marry him, eager to know if Frank approved.

I told her it was her life, and she should do what she felt was best. A little later, she told me she had decided to accept.

In Venice, they went to an opera production of *Tosca* and visited museums, even getting to meet with Peggy Guggenheim. But Lind's spirits abruptly changed when she received a letter at American Express from Francois saying the whole thing had been a mistake and he was withdrawing his proposal. Frank remembers, "Lind took it bravely, and I never saw her shed a tear."

~ 9 ~

After my conversation with the adoption agency, and speaking with Don about the call, I called Sophie, Lind's daughter, who lived in the South of France.

Sophie and I were close. Our communication with each other was infrequent, but when we talked, we talked for an hour. We exchanged Christmas gifts, and Sophie would occasionally send magazine articles or some small object she felt I would like. I was the closest family member Sophie had since she lost her mother and father.

I plunged right in. "Sophie, I have some very exciting news that may come as a shock, but a happy one, I think. Did your mom tell you she had a son and gave him up for adoption?

"No. No. Really? No. I never heard—she never told me," Sophie said. There was a long pause. "So, you are saying I have a brother?"

"Yes, you have a brother. His name is John. He has a wife, three children, and is a geologist. I'll tell you more when I know more. I can't wait to talk with him."

Sophie was upset during the rest of the call, upset that her mom had not told her. Definitely the same feeling I had, the more I thought about it. But I was mostly sad that Lind wasn't alive to meet him.

In France, Lind found a job as an English teacher at SUD-AVIATION. It was the company that, along with the British Aircraft Corporation, developed the Concorde as well as helicopters. Jean Paul Coutou, or JP, a director at Niger-Français, an import export business, was encouraged to learn English. He and a colleague joined her class. JP became very smitten with this attractive American. Lind began to feel the same for him. She continued teaching until October 29, 1965. On Christmas Eve, JP asked her to marry him.

JP had been married and divorced but had no children. He was also twelve years older than Lind. Though he learned to speak a bit of English in her class, he was not comfortable with the language. He encouraged her to speak French, which was fine with my sister. She was becoming so fluent, she wrote Mom, that she now dreamed in French.

When they got on the phone to call our parents with the news they were marrying, JP said, "I kiss you," which tickled Mom. She then liked him right away.

Lind said she fell in love with Jean Paul because he reminded her so much of Dad. I thought that comment curious. When I met him the next year, he didn't seem a bit like our dad. Looking back now, I think I get it: both men had old-fashioned ideas about men and women, husbands and wives, and the man's roll as head of household in a marriage. I doubt my sister realized at the time that that was the marriage she would have. Or maybe in the beginning that was the marriage she craved.

Evidently, Mom wrote Frank in Chapel Hill to tell him of Lind's marriage and to ask if he had any family silver of Lind's. He wrote her back on UNC English Department letterhead.

> *Dear Mrs. Earle,*
>
> *Received your card yesterday. Yes indeed, I and all of her friends in Chapel Hill are thrilled with Lind's news. Jean Paul sounds real nice, and I'm sure that they will both be very happy. My only regret is that I can't go over for the ceremony.*
>
> *I have her silver, and my count is as follows:*
> *8 knives*
> *1 butter spreader*
> *14 forks*
> *3 salad forks*
> *13 teaspoons*
> *1 sugar shell*
> *7 demi-tasse spoons*
> *1 cocktail fork*
>
> *I have checked with Jere Starling, and he says that he has none of it, so I suppose that the above accounts for it. I assume that she'll see about taking it back with her when she comes this summer, since the customs regulations for mailing silver, even used silver, are probably a little complicated. However, if you or she would like me to mail it, I'll be happy to. Come by to see me when you're in Chapel Hill—seriously.*
>
> *Best wishes, Frank Nye*

Frank later wrote of their wedding:

Henri Behar, a friend of Francois's and mine had also become close to Lind. Henri, who was flamboyantly gay, was a film critic, New York cultural correspondent for a French newspaper, and also wrote a history of the Cannes Film Festival. Lind did not invite Henri to her wedding reception, and it seemed to my other friends that he wasn't invited because JP did not approve of him and was afraid that his family would wonder what sort of woman he was marrying if she had friends like that. Anyway, several of Lind's friends boycotted Lind's wedding because she had snubbed Henri.

John Davis was almost nine when Lind, twenty-nine, and Jean Paul, forty-one, were married in a French civil service at the *mairie*, or town hall, January 21, 1966. Since JP was a divorced Catholic, it would have been difficult for them to get married in the church. I'm also pretty sure that Lind was agnostic and JP too. Mom and Dad did not go over for the wedding, nor did Rick or I. Lind discouraged us from coming. It was a civil wedding with just a few friends invited to the reception. It was expensive to fly, and Mom was petrified of airplanes. Lind promised they would visit us a few months later.

In Lind and JP's wedding portrait, the Band-Aid on Lind's leg reminds me of my favorite childhood photo of her with skinned knees and a toy rifle. (See the photos on the following page.) I like to think Lind's childhood spirit was alive and well in my sister on her wedding day.

Above, Lind, seven years old, with Mom behind her. At right, Lind and JP on their wedding day, with his parents, JP's close friends. and work colleagues.

After a honeymoon skiing in the French Alps, Lind and JP returned to his apartment at 123 rue Léon-Maurice Nordmann, Paris 13.

When they arrived for their visit, Lind was four months pregnant. Our parents gave them a party in our backyard. The article in *The Salisbury Post* said that both grandmothers attended, as well as our brother and his wife, Anne, and friends of mine from high school helped serve. Many of our parents' friends came from out of town. Afterward, Lind and JP planned to visit friends in Lynchburg and Chapel Hill. That was one of only two times Jean Paul came to the United States, though he always said he loved his American Earle

Lind and Jean Paul in our parent's backyard the summer after they were married.

family better than his own family in France.

I was very smitten with JP too. When he spoke his broken English to us, he was charming and always smiling. I was happy for my sister, I'm sure. But again, our lives hardly crossed. That would change as I got older.

I recently found a letter dated October of that year. Lind wrote to our parents after she and JP had returned to Paris. Mom had written Lind that she and Dad were hosting their gourmet club and wondered if she had any ideas about what they should serve. Lind wrote back to them.

> *Dear Folks,*
>
> *Enjoyed your letter. Had hoped you'd say something about our boxes. I have cleaned out the big cabinet to make room for everything. Will you pay for shipping from there and let us pay you back? That would help us out as we are completely broke. Do let me know.*
>
> *Merm, I don't know what to give you as a gourmet menu. I never fix anything so special. I have oysters on the half shell with lemon quarters; brown bread and butter; then a standing roast of lamb; then*

a platter of cheeses, which don't exist in the states;
salad; then dessert. You see that it's not very snazzy.

Lind followed that comment with a recipe for soufflé au citron, which was complicated. She continued:

I had a man fix some shelves that had fallen down,
and he's going to make the stand for Mogrador [her
Japanese statue], and maybe shelves for the records
if it's cheap enough. I washed the walls behind the
stove. Made watercress soup and made so much
that I gave half to the concierge. I've been reading a
lot of Balzac lately. We went to see the film Doctor
Zhivago last Friday. It's really good.

Saw also Baby Doll, the film from Tennessee
Williams's book; do you remember we saw it in the
drive-in? JP really liked it. I've taken to wearing
knee socks: nice and warm and more comfortable
than stockings every day.

Thanks anyway, but I've had Frank's address for
months. We do write each other, you know.

JP keeps saying, "Don't you let Sophie come
early." Don't know why he is so afraid or what of
a premature baby. Probably because they're uglier!
Made reservations at the private clinic, formerly a
château and very nice. In fact, that should be for us!
They keep you for 8! days. The concierge has agreed
to help out. JP wants to ask Manou and Papa—his
parents—to give us the basic baby things for Xmas,
to save us that expense! Ok with me! Almost 4
months to go! Gosh, it's long. Sophie is very acrobat-
ic; she keeps me company! (The car is blocked in this
week by work on the ceiling, or else I'd have gone to

Paris visiting or something; too lazy to go by train!)
    *Well, I haven't much news! We are both fine and
happy and hope you all are the same. Hope to have
news of the boxes soon. Give Bam a big kiss for us.*
    Much love to all,
    Lind

There are several things that stand out to me in Lind's
letter. Of course, she said she never fixed anything special
then listed the very special foods she served and mentioned
the cheeses she knew we didn't have. Most surprising
though is that she mentioned they had no money—twice.
I wonder if JP was paying alimony to his first wife and that
could be the issue. He had no children from his first marriage. Or maybe it was the cost of their recent trip to the
States? They soon would buy a wonderful house in Saint-
Prix. Did JP's parents help pay for that? All very curious.

Sophie Jeanne Henriette Coutou was born into our family February 8, 1967. Lind gently made it clear to Mom
that Sophie was named after JP's mother, Henriette—not
Harriett, my first name and my great aunt's name. It didn't
hurt my feelings. I had begged my parents to call me by my
middle name, Vaughan, when I started grade school, because my brother loved to call me "Harri-idiot." But I could
tell Mom was disappointed. Aunt Harriett, Mom's father's
only sister, was Mom's favorite aunt and had left her silver
service to me. I guess she felt at least one of Sophie's names
should have been from our side of the family.
    Lind's love of music came naturally. Our mother, Rosalind
Thomas Johnson, born in Savannah, Georgia on July 1, 1911,
dreamed of becoming a concert pianist. She was an excellent

student and played piano at the Episcopal Church, though she was occasionally criticized for jazzing up the hymns.

Mom intended to get a music degree at Brenau College in Gainesville, Georgia. But before the second year was up, the Depression intervened, crippling her father's dental-supply business. Her dad, she told me "just showed up" and said, "Pack your things, you are coming home." Mom always regretted that she didn't apply for a scholarship which she felt she would have won.

Home from Brenau College, she began working in Rich's department store in Savannah as a salesclerk. Dad had moved to Savannah after college to work for Firestone Tire. He had been born in Gordonsville, Virginia, also in 1911, attended Fishburne Military School and had a business degree from what is now North Carolina State University.

They met at a dance at the Desoto Hotel, known as the center of social life in Savannah. It was love at first sight for her. Dad took a little longer. He was quite a ladies' man, very handsome, full of fun and laughter, and a terrific dancer.

After Mom and Dad were married on November 7, 1936, at St. John's Episcopal Church in Savannah, they moved to Lynchburg, Virginia.

Even though Dad had been born in Virginia, he had grown up in Salisbury, so when his father asked him to come to Salisbury to help him in his business, Dad readily agreed. As a young, attractive couple with a son and daughter—and eventually me—it did not take long for them to adjust to their new home. St. Luke's Episcopal Church was the center of our family life. Mom volunteered, we sang in the choir and attended Episcopal Youth Community and church camp, and Dad was on the vestry. He was also in the Rotary Club, served as a city councilman, and later mayor pro tem.

— 10 —

In November 2009, John Davis wrote an email addressed to "my birth mother's family." In it, he wrote:

I was born March 22, 1957, in Washington, DC, I know my mother named me James Earle before she gave me up for adoption. I was told the middle name she gave me was a family name from the Earle side, but at this point, I do not know that middle name. I was brought to the Greensboro Children's Home within a couple of weeks of birth. I was then placed with an adoptive family around the first of May of that year. My adoptive parents were an Episcopal priest and a homemaker. I also had an older adoptive sister. I spent my childhood in North Carolina and then went to boarding school in Virginia for high school. I went to college and graduate school at North Carolina universities.

I did contact the Greensboro Children's Home twenty years ago, but at that time they were not allowed to give out information to either adoptees or birth parents. The law has just recently changed.

I am a professional geologist and environmental consultant. I love music and literature, especially southern fiction, and I'm also interested in old house architecture. I am healthy, although I do have asthma. My thirteen-year-old daughter also has asthma. I am married and have three beautiful children, a son aged fifteen; a daughter, aged thirteen; and our youngest daughter is ten years old. My wife is, happily, a stay-at-home mom.

I also want you to know that I did have loving, stable adoptive parents and was given many opportunities in life with many cousins and extended family. I am happy and am described as easy-going and friendly. But I have always felt that something was missing for me, not knowing anything about my birth parents. I would love to know who my mother really was as a person. What her likes and dislikes were and her dreams for her own life.

Sincerely,

John

John also included several photos of himself, his wife, and his children. I immediately sent the letter and photos to my brother, his daughters, and to Sophie. Everyone was thrilled—including Sophie, but she was still terribly hurt, a little angry, and confused as to why her mother kept this secret from her.

When I emailed John and told him how happy we were he found us, he replied:

Vaughan,

Thank you so much for your warm and welcoming words and acceptance of me. It's such a thrill to find my family and to know more about where I came from.

I wish I could have found her a long time ago. Now, I have the opportunity to get to know Lind through you and Sophie, and I greatly look forward to that.

You won't believe this. I already have a picture of your mom. My wife's stepfather has an aunt that lived in Salisbury for many years back in the '50s and '60s. He asked Aunt Clara (Childs) if she knew the Earles, and she said her best friend was Roz Earle. Clara was a portrait painter. She also said her best subject was Vaughan, the youngest. She promptly pulled out a picture of both herself and Roz, your mom, in the Salisbury Post *taken in 1985. And the world gets smaller…*

Please send Sophie's contact info. I would like to send her a note. I can't wait to meet you and the rest of the family. The picture you sent of the nieces and nephews in front of the fireplace, can I assume the middle person is Sophie? She looks like the pictures of Lind. I will write and send more pictures soon.

Thanks, hugs to all.

In March of 2015, before the Zoom call with CHS but after I had learned about and met John, I started to write down all I could remember about Lind, hoping to make sense of her life. I needed to talk with someone who knew her in high school. I emailed Wyndham Robertson to ask if she would tell me anything she could remember about my sister. Wyndham responded and I replied to her in turn:

Wyndham,

It is terrific to hear back from you. My husband and I live in Charlotte and have two grown sons. Don was in the wine business working for Mondavi for many years. I was in the TV commercial business as executive producer with a film company. I am painting and doing photography. He's playing a lot of golf and baking bread. We just got back from Cuba through the College of Charleston and Cuba Educational Tours. We learned so much and have some terrific photos.

Lind's birth son John found us four years ago, and that is what started me writing about her. I really didn't know much about Lind, since I was 12 years younger. Unfortunately, her son was only able to connect with us after she had died, so I never knew or got to talk with her about it.

We love him already and his wonderful family, and Lind's daughter Sophie is thrilled to know she has a brother.

Vaughan

Wyndham was just as surprised about Lind having a baby as I had been and hadn't known a thing. She had graduated a year earlier than Lind and was not living in Salisbury at the time. She had known Jim Rabon very well when they were all in high school and said he was a great guy.

She suggested we meet in Salisbury for dinner when she would be there for a meeting, as well as visiting friends. Don and I met her at a small, popular Italian restaurant named Chef Santos. I told her what John had told me— that he had always wanted to see his records and when the laws finally changed, he petitioned to have them opened. That was how he found his father, Jim, and then me. I told her how nice John seemed and what a great family he had. She asked who his adoptive parents were.

"Johnny and Sarah Davis. He was an Episcopalian minister and—"

She stopped me there. "Really? I knew them well! They were friends of my friend Betty Kenan."

The news was jaw dropping, so just to be certain, Wyndham picked up her cell phone and called Betty from the table. Yes, Betty confirmed, the Davises indeed had an adopted son, John, whom she had known since childhood.

When Wyndham hung up, she said, "This is amazing. We need to all get together as soon as possible in Chapel Hill."

After meeting in Salisbury and then later in Chapel Hill with Betty, John, John's wife, Don, and me, Wyndham became an enthusiastic supporter of my writing Lind's story.

— II —

In July of 1967, after I graduated from high school, Mom and Dad sent me to spend a month with my sister and to attend Sophie's christening. I flew from Charlotte to La Guardia, then took a helicopter to the JFK Airport for the overnight flight.

When I finally walked onto the plane, I saw seats jammed with backpackers, moms, and crying babies. I had Mom's portable Singer sewing machine with me because Lind had requested it. Since it wouldn't fit in the overhead bin, I kept it under my feet. I doubt that would be allowed today.

I flew the cheapest flight Dad could find, Icelandic Air. It didn't matter to me. It was all very exciting. This was my first flight ever, and I loved everything about it. I remember writing poems and drawing pictures in my journal during the flight, fascinated at being above the clouds, while smokers puffed away in the last eight rows.

At midflight, we stopped to refuel in Reykjavik, where we were allowed to de-plane and visit the gift shop. I bought a white sheepskin for seven dollars to use as a rug back home in my room. It was perfect to snuggle in for the rest of the overnight flight. We then flew to Luxembourg. I boarded a bus for a four-hour ride to the center of Paris, where my sister picked me up. The combination of sleeplessness, jetlag, the plane ride, the bus ride, and anxiety about the trip must have overwhelmed me. When I finally crawled into bed at Lind and Jean Paul's apartment, I slept for two days. Then I awoke to the magnificent new world of Paris.

The contrast between Salisbury and Paris was mind-boggling. Salisbury was a small town with a population of about 28,000. The downtown was two blocks of Innes Street and two blocks of Main Street on either side of the square. I was also struck at that age by the differences in food. Mom bought groceries at the A&P or Food Town, which later became Food Lion, owned by the Ketners, a local family. To me, groceries were cans of food in the cabinet, a freezer packed with frozen vegetables, frozen steaks wrapped in bacon, and fluffy dinner rolls.

In Paris, Lind and I visited the bakery every day for the evening meal, toasting leftovers for breakfast in the morning. After the bakery, we stopped at the large farmers market for fresh vegetables and fish or went to the butcher shop for meat. Lind's refrigerator was tiny, shorter than my five-foot-five frame, and had a freezer only large enough for two little ice trays—which they never used. Every morning, we toasted baguettes, slathered them with butter and jam, and sipped large mugs of hot sugared tea. We never ate eggs for breakfast; omelets were made at supper time. The mayonnaise and mustard were in little tubes you squeezed, like toothpaste. I loved that. To me, it was so different, so romantic. I became convinced France was the best place to live and Paris was the most beautiful city in the world.

Even though a justice of the peace had married Lind and JP, it was *de rigueur* in his family and ours that a child be baptized. So, cute-as-pie, six-month-old Sophie had a traditional christening, complete with long white baptismal gown, lacy little cap, and adoring parents, godparents, and aunt—me—to stand up for her. Lind and JP asked their closest friends at the time, Georges, who worked with JP, and his wife Nicole to be Sophie's godparents.

I loved being around Georges, a funny and flirty French-man who insisted I call him *gros ours en peluche*—big teddy bear—and I was *petit ours en peluche*—little teddy bear. I sat in the front seat of his fancy Citroën on the way to the church. He drove a little fast and recklessly, his wife thought, but I found it fun. I didn't feel that comfortable around Ni-cole, who was very reserved. Lind said the French gener-ally take a long time to include foreigners in their group of friends—and, she added, Nicole did her ironing while wearing pearls, designer suits, and heels. I noticed, when she took off her jacket later, she didn't shave her underarms. I found that contrast of hairy underarms with her stylish dress and perfect image a strange contradiction, but Lind just laughed. "Women not shaving in France is very normal."

Mom had made clothes for me for the trip, and she had bought me the most adorable dark green and white dotted Swiss dress for the christening. Lind was her usual elegant self. Sophie looked precious and didn't fuss at all when the priest holding her made the sign of the cross on her fore-head and let some of the holy water run into her eyes.

After the service, Lind and JP invited everyone back to their apartment for champagne and hors d'oeuvres.

They gave candy-coated almonds as party favors, a French tradition. The five almonds wrapped in pink paper and tied with pink ribbon stood for wishing the child health, pros-perity, longevity, fertility, and happiness. Thankfully, Lind had plenty more, because I fell in love with those almonds.

Munching on those and all the baguettes, butter, jam, and chocolate, I gained a few pounds on my trip that summer.

Though I'd never played tennis, Lind bought me a white tennis skirt and top to wear when we visited their racquetball club. After whacking the tennis ball a few times, I watched Sophie while she slept in her stroller in the warm, late-morning sunshine. When we went to the club, Lind often prepared a lunch of roast beef, bone in and carved at the picnic table by JP; a French-style salad of just lettuce, oil, and lemon juice; and potato chips. We used cloth napkins, china plates, and bottled water, another new experience for me. Everything they did felt so romantic, so special.

One day while Lind prepared our morning baguettes, she told me she stayed thin by toasting her bread, which reduced the calories. I had never heard that and thought it was ridiculous. I didn't say that to her though. A better reason she stayed thin, I thought silently, was because of her endless smoking and eating like a bird. Later, she admitted to me that she had been wrong.

It also makes me think of the way Mom said Lind was fed as a baby. Doctors in the '30s and '40s recommended to mothers that babies be bathed, played with, and fed on a set schedule. Mom said Lind cried a lot as a baby, and yet Mom didn't feed her if it was not the scheduled time. She thought Lind had been constantly hungry, and Mom felt guilty about it.

Mom said it was different when I came along. She fed me whenever I acted hungry. No set schedules for me. I was one fat and happy baby.

Several days later, we all went to Saint-Jean-de-Luz, located in Basque country on the Atlantic coast near Spain.

Lind took Sophie on the train, and JP and I drove in his car. Our drive took seven hours and was uncomfortable for me, and probably JP too, since neither of us could communicate very well. Occasionally, he let out a few expletives about other drivers. "*Zut alors, merde, si bête, imbecile.*" "Damn then, shit, so stupid, idiot." I laughed each time, and that seemed to make him happy. At lunch, we stopped for a roadside picnic of cheese and bread. Mostly, as we traveled that day, we just smiled at each other.

In Saint-Jean-de-Luz, we stayed in Hotel De La Plage with a view of the bay and the ocean. Lind and JP shared a room with Sophie, and I had the room across the hall. My sister craved the warmth of the sun, so most days we spent on the beach. We all got darker and darker, even six-month-old Sophie. At that time, there were no warnings about sun causing skin cancer.

Lind signed me up for sailing lessons. The other student and the instructor spoke a little English, which helped a lot. At the end of the week, we were both presented our official sailing diplomas.

After dinners, usually in the hotel since it was all-inclusive, JP stayed in their room to put Sophie to bed while my sister and I walked to the village square and sat on the terrace of a café, hoping I would find some young people to hang out with at night. A small band played, and lots of locals and tourists gathered to drink and mingle. I learned to love Pernod, a drink that tasted like licorice. Lind only drank tea and made sure I added lots of water to my glass of Pernod.

After a few uneventful nights, a young German, about twenty, introduced himself. He seemed intrigued I was American and asked if I'd join him and meet his friends. Lind, I'm sure, was relieved she no longer had to babysit me and could stay at the hotel with JP and Sophie. Lind set no curfew or made demands on what I should do or where I should go, and I had the most liberating and adventurous three weeks of my life.

My new-found friends—two French and three German—were on vacation and enjoying their freedom too. One of the girls spoke no English, and I got the impression she didn't like an American tagging along, but the German boy spoke English well and was protective of me. Several times during the next few weeks, we piled into a beat-up 1955 Citroën, crossing the border into San Sebastian, Spain, where the bars offered free tapas if we purchased drinks.

On July 14, Bastille Day, we drove to the town of Bayonne and danced in the streets, singing along with others as we walked from bar to bar giving toast after toast to French liberation. I crawled into bed that night as the sun rose, reflecting on how different France was—people bursting into song in bars or on the street and strangers sitting together in restaurants, locking arms and laughing. I couldn't picture that happening back in Salisbury. I loved it. I loved France.

That trip changed me. As soon as I got back home, I impulsively broke up with my high school boyfriend. I wanted a fresh start when I got to college, a chance to explore new places and meet new people, or so I thought. But I found out rather quickly I was still that small-town girl heavily influenced by her parents.

～ 12 ～

That fall of '67, I packed up to attend St. Mary's College in Raleigh for my freshman year. My parents wanted me in a two-year school, and my brother recommended it to them for me. I was placed in a small dorm called West Rock, off the left wing of the school. Thoughts of France were quickly replaced by college life—classes, new friends, and dating became my focus.

My roommate, Jill, was from Washington, North Carolina. Her parents had divorced, and she was estranged from her father. We talked a lot about it, though at the time, I didn't know many divorced parents and was probably no help. Jill had terrible menstrual cramps; several days a month, she would stay in bed all day with the curtains closed, the lights off, and the radiator turned up high. Those weeks I tried to stay out of our room as much as possible to let her rest. Still she couldn't have been a better roommate. While we sat on our beds and studied, we ate canned Vienna sausages, corned beef, bags of potato chips, and too many other junk foods. We both put on the college freshman ten pounds, fortunately losing it over the spring semester. Besides chatting and laughing about some of our dates, one of my favorite times was when we both brought our pig fetus to the room to dissect over a weekend.

We were a crazy mix of girls in our tiny two-story dorm. One had terrible kidney stones. She suffered through them in her room and never did go to the hospital. Not once. Another West Rock girl was the sweetheart of Sigma Chi. She encouraged me to start smoking, so we could go behind the cafeteria and smoke together. I regretted that. It seemed a lot of college students smoked at that time.

There were just fourteen of us in West Rock. Isolated from the rest of the students living on halls with thirty to forty girls, we felt like outcasts, so we banded together. Going through magazines one day, I found photos of the cast of *Oliver* playing on Broadway. Amazed at how each of the boy actors looked exactly like one of us in the dorm, I cut out the photos and wrote in our respective names, taping the photos to our dorm-room wall. We became the abandoned and forgotten "boys" of West Rock, out for fun and maybe even a little mischief.

Two sophomore girls at St. Mary's were from Salisbury and took me on as their project, helping me change my high school wardrobe into one more appropriate for fraternity parties. They introduced me to the PIKA and SAE fraternities at NC State and kept me busy on blind dates. I did eventually find a nice guy to date from the SAE house and became one of their "little sisters."

I never had a problem with academics in high school. But that changed in college. I found the classes much harder at St. Mary's. Many of the girls there had gone to private high schools and were way ahead of me when it came to writing English papers and knowing how to study. Footnotes? What the heck were they? My first semester, I received a

D in English and an F on a paper I wrote. Obviously, I was not blessed with my sister's academic intelligence.

I needed to redeem myself with my English professor. I thought about a long poem I'd written in high school. During my senior year, a girlfriend and I took my mom's Cadillac and drove to Kannapolis to attend a KKK rally. We were more curious than anything, and it never occurred to us to be scared or that police might take down my mom's license number to keep on file. We never told anyone, and my parents never found out.

We were appalled by what we saw and heard at that rally. Big bellied, uneducated white men in white robes and white pointed hats burned crosses, used crude language, their wives shaking their heads in agreement and young children running wild. I could not stop thinking about it. I wrote a long poem, quoting some of their mean-spirited speeches, as well as describing unsettling visuals from the rally.

I showed my English professor at St. Mary's the poem I'd written, sure she would recognize my creativity and give me at least a C. When, a month later, I got the nerve to ask what she thought, and to get it back, she couldn't find it. I bet she never read it. I did get a C, but that felt like the end of my blooming poetic and literary career. I turned toward a more social life.

In the spring of 1968, I received an invitation to the North Carolina Debutante Ball, the same early fall event Lind had attended twelve years before me. I had great fun traveling all over the state to parties and picnics and imagining Lind doing the same. Though now, decades later, I know she was probably not having the unbridled fun I was having that summer.

The five debutantes from Salisbury gave a party at the Salisbury Country Club. Several wealthier debs in the state had much bigger parties with more expensive bands like Major Lance, The Drifters, or The Tams, and the parties included a midnight breakfast. But I didn't care. Our party was a great success, and we all had a wonderful night.

One Sunday after the service at St. Luke's Episcopal Church, I vaguely remember Mom stopping Blanche Robertson and thanking her. Mrs. Robertson was on the committee that chose the debutantes each year, though that was supposed to be a secret. I assume now that Mother thought I wouldn't be chosen after what had happened with Lind, but at the time, I knew nothing of my sister's pregnancy. Neither Mother nor Dad had ever said a word to me.

Dad was my escort to the ball in Raleigh. Lind had three good-looking men when she was a deb. The rules had changed, and they requested we ask our fathers, thank goodness. It made sense to me. My sister might have been able to handle three men at one time, but that was not for me.

The debs and their families stayed at the Sir Walter Raleigh Hotel for the dance. Mom smoked cigarettes and ate diet foods for months in advance to lose weight. She really did look lovely. And Dad made the absolute best dancing partner.

My second year at St. Mary's, I was chosen as a senior counselor for the freshman girls in one of the dorms. Some of my friends began smoking pot, and one even dropped acid. Though I was not a prude, I was scared of drugs and did not want to get involved. I was not getting along with my SAE boyfriend and was concerned about my grades. I was not coping well. I became nervous and depressed and asked Mom and Dad if I could come home.

Dad grudgingly agreed but was not a bit happy about losing that semester's tuition. I think now, my parents must have been holding their breath about me. I was asking to leave college around Thanksgiving my sophomore year—virtually the same time Lind had left Sullins, though not for the same reason. My parents wouldn't have been able to handle it if I had become pregnant like Lind. I knew none of that at the time. I just felt bad about leaving school and disappointing them.

After John and I had emailed several times, we decided to meet in Salisbury.

He wanted me to show him around town—places Lind frequented while in high school. He wanted to see the house his mother grew up in, the high school she went to, the gravesite where our parents were buried. Then he would follow me back to Charlotte and spend the weekend with our family.

When I saw the middle-aged man walking into the Starbucks on Innes Street in Salisbury, I saw my brother. I would have recognized my nephew anywhere. We hugged immediately, both of us excited and nervous. He sat across from me, and I just stared—his curly dark hair, the way he crossed his legs, the way he kept his reading glasses down on his nose, his body type, his big fat thumbs—all Earle family markers. He was identical to my brother and father in so many ways.

During that first meeting in Salisbury, I tried to play family tour guide and historian, showing John our hometown as best I could. But again, I could only fill in details from my perspective, since I was so much younger than my sister and I had been kept in the dark for so long.

First, we went by our old home on Marsh Street. It looked so small and a little run down. The neighborhood had been a great one to grow up in, with lots of kids of all ages. I told John that my dad's parents—Bam and Pop—had lived in a big house next door, which was now gone. We drove by Boyden High School, and I mentioned that my sister was a co-chief cheerleader and was very popular.

I took John by the old Blackwelder's Barbeque, where I was sure his mom's generation, as well as mine, hung out as teenagers after Friday night ball games. I usually had the BBQ salad with Thousand Island dressing or the crispy hush puppies with ketchup. We drove through the parking lot of Al's Night Hawk, where the older high school athletes sat on Cheerwine crates and drank beer on the weekends.

"Do you know my birth father?" John asked. "Have you ever met him?"

"No," I said, "I don't know anything about him."

"Let's go then," he said. "I want you to meet him. His store is just in the next parking lot."

"You're kidding."

"Wouldn't do that." He grinned.

As we turned into the parking lot off West Innes Street, John told me he had had a couple of work assignments in Salisbury, never realizing his birth mother and father had lived there. As an environmental consultant with a large firm in Virginia, John was often sent to check for underground leaks in old gas stations slated for demolition. When he was finally allowed to know who his birth father was, he realized that Jim owned a jewelry store, Windsor Gallery Fine Jewelers, in the shopping center just behind the very same gas station he surveyed.

John had not told him that we might stop by. I admitted to being nervous about meeting Jim, and about how he'd feel meeting me. I wondered if Jim held a grudge against our family. I would understand if he did. But John didn't seem worried.

"He's a great guy," he said.

Our visit was a little awkward. Jim and I were both a bit shy about meeting. But there were polite hellos and nice to meet yous. Jim was a good-looking older man in his seventies and had a great smile. I could see how Lind could have fallen for him in high school. His wife and daughter were in the store also and very friendly. Jim was quiet though, and I really couldn't blame him. I wasn't sure what to say to him either since I knew very little about what had happened. But John chatted on happily and was a great icebreaker.

After serving in the Army and losing his son to adoption, Jim stayed on in Salisbury. He married a local girl, Carol, and they had a son as well as a daughter who worked with them in the store. They had been happily married for many years when I met him. I wondered if a marriage between Jim and my sister—so enamored with travel, art, music, literature, and languages—would have worked out. But her life did not turn out that well in France, so who am I to speculate?

— 13 —

Lind was the best gift-giver ever. She loved anything miniature, and on birthdays or at Christmas, she would mail us gifts of small crèche figures, Catholic communion cards, tiny baskets, little wooden hearts, or diminutive pigs for my collection. I loved receiving those tissue-paper-wrapped wonders. Once on a postcard she sent, she had drawn over a hundred red hearts with a fine-tipped magic marker. I marveled at her patience and at the time she took making those special surprises.

She was also a faithful letter writer and wrote to Mom weekly, detailing Sophie's accomplishments and interesting tidbits about everyday life. I easily picture Lind putting on the tea kettle to boil and getting out her large, brown pottery mug with tea stains and small cracks in the porcelain. She would put several teaspoons of sugar in the mug, pour in hot water, and dip her tea bag until the tea was the color of her chocolate mug. She would go about her ritual reverently, never in a rush. Only then would she sit down at her desk in her tiny bedroom, light a Gauloise, and write a long chatty letter on thin airmail paper. I tried to be a good sister and write her back, but when a few letters came back corrected for spelling, grammar, or punctuation, I lost my enthusiasm. I decided to call her instead.

After leaving St. Mary's, I attended Catawba College, majoring in advertising and marketing, while working in a clothing store and, evenings, waiting tables in a bar. On Saturdays, I made deliveries for my dad's office supply business. Despite being busy, life in Salisbury remained lonely, and I just wasn't thrilled with the "read the textbook" marketing program. I was happy when a friend from St. Mary's asked me to share an apartment with her in Raleigh. We both got jobs in the same clothing store.

Not long after moving to our apartment, my roommate met an NC State football player and fell madly in love. I, in turn, started dating his friend. One night, out of the blue, they each proposed to us. Without really thinking, I said yes. I wrote Lind and told her about it, sending along his photo. She called shortly after and, in a strained voice, told me he was the wrong guy for me, his face had no character, and, if I was marrying him to have sex, it was the wrong reason. She said to think seriously about it, that Mom had probably driven it into my head sex was for marriage only. At the time, I couldn't imagine why she got so upset or why she thought I'd marry for sex. I did marry him and moved to Wilmington. Six months later, I broke out in hives at work. I couldn't breathe. Monk, a sweet, older coworker, rushed me to the hospital. I called my parents and asked if I could come home. I divorced the man at the end of the year. My sister had it so right.

I tried Catawba College again, majoring in theater this time, and it clicked. Though I couldn't act—too nervous to put myself out there like I'm sure Lind would have—I loved everything else, especially the other students and the professors. I designed costumes for *Once Upon a Mattress*, was assistant director for *Man of La Mancha*, and president of the Blue Masque, the theater club. I was a bit older than the other students in our junior year, but no one seemed to notice or care.

I lived at home while at Catawba, and I happily took over my sister's bedroom. Lind had convinced our parents to redo it when she was in high school. It was all her creative design. There was a built-in dresser and desk, a floor to ceiling bookcase with a few of her books and records she had left at home when she had gone to France. Across from the bookcase was a wall of sliding closet doors, and behind one of the sliding doors were drawers for her underwear and sweaters. She had left several of her cashmere sweaters, each one neatly folded in a clear plastic bag, the ends left open for air. The sweaters were beautiful soft colors. Because of her smoking, each sweater had one or two cigarette burns—probably why she left them behind. I wore them anyway. I loved those sweaters. I loved that room. I loved my sister's style.

In the years since I learned of John Davis's existence, I have begun to look back on the stages of my life by thinking about what he was doing at the same time. He was fifteen in 1972, in high school, and wondering about his birth family. His half-sister Sophie was five. And I was starting a new job in Charlotte after I had graduated early from Catawba in February of that year. I began working in a 16-millimeter film-processing lab whose headquarters were in Memphis, Tennessee. I worked in the front office and met all kinds of interesting people in the film and television business. One of those contacts led to a "girl Friday" job with a director-cameraman.

The next year I met my future husband, Don, at the Lake Apartments where we both were living. I was sharing an apartment with a girl who had also graduated from Catawba and was a stringer for WSOC-TV. We ran into Don while walking, and he invited us to a wine tasting at his apartment. At first, he showed much more interest in my blonde, buxom roommate, but he finally got smart and realized I was the one he should be asking out.

Don had come back to the states from Germany in December of 1973. As a lieutenant in the US Army, he had been a Pershing platoon commander for two years and then, with his top security clearance, spent two more years doing reliability studies of nuclear missiles for Page Communication Engineers. Because he was an only child, his mom had encouraged him to come home.

He moved to Charlotte to take two undergraduate classes at UNC-Charlotte in order to get into graduate school at UNC-Chapel Hill. Meanwhile, a fraternity brother purchased a small wine company, Vintage Distributing, in Charlotte and asked Don to run it. He agreed and never took the classes or got his master's. Vintage Distributing started importing German and other European wines and became successful. Don, as manager, did the bulk of the work.

Soon after we started dating, Don left the Lake Apartments and moved into a large house outside of town with two other UNC-CH fraternity brothers, David and Tom. Don and I were getting more serious, so not long after he left, I left and moved into the guesthouse on the property.

We all lived there for free since the estate was held by the bank Tom worked for. It was once owned by the family that built the Charlotte Hotel, and the property boasted a swimming pool, stables, a pond, fruit trees, and acreage. A cleaning lady, Edna, came with the property and lived in a house nearby. The house had a cat we named Sourdough and a peacock we named Gilbert. David invented our own ghost for the house he called Plaid Man.

From the large, gray slate patio and kitchen window, we could see the skyline of Charlotte. We had terrific parties on that patio; it was a sad day for all of us when the bank sold the property.

My parents came only once for the day, and we had fun showing them around. I wish my brother and sister could have seen the house. Both of them would have loved it too. But during the time we all lived there, neither Lind nor Rick ever came close to Charlotte.

Today the Bland Estate is gone, so swallowed up by a housing development that it is impossible to see where the house had been. We have tried, several times, but we have never found it.

My brother Rick, his wife Anne, and their daughter Carolyn had been living in Greensboro. After a couple of years, he got a job at Cincinnati Fan and Ventilator and they moved to Cincinnati where their second daughter, Merrick, was born. Merrick was four and Carolyn six when Rick and Anne divorced in 1974; soon after, my brother married his second wife, Tass. I remember the day Rick told Mom and Dad he was marrying again. Dad said, "That's too bad, I really liked the first one." But Dad and all of us grew to love his second wife too. Tass had four children of her own, and for a few years, my brother's daughters also lived with them in Cincinnati. My brother ended up with six children. Hard for me to believe.

Interestingly, my brother recently told me that our parents confessed they had considered a divorce around the same time he was divorcing. Another thing I never knew! Was something wrong with me? I must have been so naïve. I wonder how much I knew about anything in our family.

Early in 1975, Don and I became engaged. I believe the timing was right for both of us. He was thirty-one and I was twenty-six. I thought he looked like Robert Redford. He said he liked my short skirts and curly red hair. He drove a red Porsche 911T he had brought back with him from Germany. We had a lot of fun in that car. We especially loved autocross competitions, which we did with the Sports Car Club of America group in and around Charlotte. Don and I both liked to drive a fast car. I loved the rumble of the engine. Don said that when we were dating, he was amazed by how I could maneuver in the traffic all the way into town. When I was moving to Charlotte after graduating from college, Dad had given me a denim-upholstered Gremlin, which embarrassed me. Not a car I would have chosen. Definitely not sexy like the BMW I was wanting, but it did the job of getting around in traffic.

These were the years of brown bagging in Charlotte. Liquor laws did not allow restaurants to sell alcohol, so diners took their own bottles in brown bags. One of our favorite memories is of the bar at the El Villa restaurant on Providence Road. It had been a Tuscan-style home but was rented to a Mrs. Judy Lindsay who made it into a high-end restaurant with a downstairs bar. In the bar, there were lockers you could purchase to store your liquor. The bartender was Doug Clark, who was quite a personality. He wore a Panama hat. The bar had a piano, and women were known to dance on it late in the evenings. I might have danced on it once. But I was usually reserved around a crowd of people.

Another place we loved to go, though saved for special occasions, was Café Eugene. The chef, Steve Hermann, prepared the best duck we have ever eaten. The meat was juicy and the skin crisp. The orange sauce was incredible. Dessert for birthdays and anniversaries was an old favorite, Baked Alaska. Steve Hermann had drug issues and had to close the restaurant. Sad day for us. Reading this now, it seems we loved good food and fast cars. But there were other things we wanted to do.

I wrote my sister that Don and I were getting married, enclosing his photo, curious to see if she would approve of this one. This time she called to say he looked like the perfect man for me.

Before we married, we searched for a house we could afford, choosing to scout the countryside since we felt homes in Charlotte too expensive. At that time, Don was making $7,000 a year in the wine import business. I had recently gotten the new job as a secretary, typist, make-up stylist, script supervisor, and set stylist with a director-cameraman and made about $3,600 a year.

Don and I wanted a farmhouse with some land and woods to walk in, where I could gather moss and stones, and we could cut down our own cedar tree at Christmas. After days spent touring uninspiring houses in the nearby towns of Mineral Springs and Monroe, the Realtor finally took me to a hundred-year-old farmhouse on Providence Road in Weddington, about twenty miles south of Charlotte in Union County. I found it charming, falling in love immediately. Don was sick in bed with the flu and a 101-degree temperature when I called to tell him that "this is the house!"

"You have to come see this house. It's perfect—twelve-foot ceilings, wide heart-pine floorboards. The Realtor says there is a fireplace in the kitchen covered up with sheet rock. The windows in the dining room and living room go all the way to the floor. There's an old open shed in the back and a place for you to have a workshop. It is so great, just perfect. Please come now."

"But I'm sick as a dog," he moaned.

"What if we lose it? What if somebody gets here first and buys it?"

"Is the real estate woman there?"

"Yes, right beside me."

"Well, I guess the price of the house just went up," he sighed.

"Oh, yes. Well. It's thirty-six thousand. Is that too much?"

We bought the house and rented it back to the owners for three months until after our wedding.

Don and I married on August 2, 1975, at the church I grew up in, St. Luke's Episcopal. Don had never been baptized. Even though his mother never missed a Sunday going to church, she wanted him to be the one to make that decision. When we went to our meeting with Uly Harrison Gooch, our rector, we were informed that we could not get married unless Don was baptized. So, the next day, he was.

Lind and Sophie flew over from France for the wedding. Lind, thirty-seven, was my matron of honor and Sophie, eight, our flower girl. Don had practically his entire Phi Gam fraternity for ushers. The reception was at my parents' house on Richmond Road. My parents employed a man named Will as a handyman. Mom and Will spent the hot August morning putting wet newspapers on the impatiens in the backyard to keep them from wilting. During the reception, all twelve of Don's ushers dragged him upstairs to one of the bedrooms and wrote his former girlfriends' names in Magic Marker all over his body. They made up a few extra names to cover his whole chest and back. Typical of my dad, halfway through the reception, he took off his tux pants and put on shorts. Granted, it was hot. If it had been later in the evening, he probably would have started blinking the lights for everyone to go home.

I was so wrapped up in the wedding and getting ready for the honeymoon that I hardly had any time to spend with Lind and Sophie. But I know Mom and Dad loved having them there for a few calmer days.

Matron of honor Lind and flower girl Sophie coming out of the church after our wedding. The other little girl is Jane, one of Tass's daughters.

Below: Don and me at our reception.

I don't know what we were thinking when we chose to honeymoon in New Orleans in August, but despite the heat it was mostly fabulous. Lind told me before we left that she had gone to Mardi Gras once, was nearly trampled to death, hated the rowdy crowds, and wouldn't go back for anything.

Our hotel, Maison de Ville, was located in the French Quarter and backed up to the Court of Two Sisters restaurant. Our room had a small balcony, and Don and I sat there in the mornings having coffee, watching the street cleaners water down the stink from Bourbon Street. Other days, we had breakfast in the small, secluded courtyard of the hotel, feeding bits of our croissants to the seemingly hundreds of scruffy little brown sparrows.

I have always loved antiques, old buildings, and junk stores. And I'm fascinated by stories of vampires, voodoo, astrology, and auras. I was crazy about New Orleans. I dragged Don all over the back streets looking for little out-of-the-way shops. It was definitely not his interest, but he went along, always finding a bench outside the shop to sit on.

One night we rode the streetcar out St. Charles to Commander's Palace in the Garden District for dinner. Another night we took a ferry across the Mississippi to Le Ruth's, a five-star restaurant in Gretna that closed in 1991. We ate at Brennan's and had the famous bananas Foster for dessert.

When we got back home Don, who loved to cook, had to make bananas Foster trying different rums and ice creams. This went on for several weeks. That made me happy, I have to say.

Despite the humid heat and palmetto bugs crunching under foot at night, we had a wonderful honeymoon. Later, New Orleans would become one of the cities Don called on with the new company he worked for, Somerset Wine. If I could get away and go with him on his sales trips, I would spend the day exploring. I loved New Orleans then and felt safe. The last time we visited it had changed, and I was not as comfortable exploring alone.

When we returned from our honeymoon, Dad and Will drove back and forth from Salisbury to Weddington, helping us move furniture into our little farmhouse. Dad had been treated recently for prostate cancer, and I caught him taking quite a few swigs of the whiskey he hid in our wine bar. I hadn't realized the seriousness of his condition until then, and it scared me. Still, I had no idea how soon I would lose my dad.

～ 15 ～

Don and I were eager to get in some travel before having children, and his contacts in the wine business helped with introductions to well-known wine makers in France and Germany. In September 1977 we flew over, staying first in Paris with Lind, Jean Paul, and Sophie. They were living north of the Seine in Saint-Prix, fifteen kilometers outside the city of Paris. Saint-Prix was near the Montmorency Forest, a popular hiking area.

The house was on a hill surrounded by a stone privacy wall. There was a view of the Eiffel Tower and the city below from the back patio and garden. It was a three-story house with a one-room stone tower where we slept. There was one bathroom we all shared on the second floor, as well as a small powder room on the first floor. The house was small by American standards, but Lind had decorated it with her artistic flair. Over the cinnamon-colored leather sofa in the main room was a fabric hanging of an abstract landscape she had sewn using whites, beiges, and small-patterned material.

Lind and JP threw a party for us, serving lots and lots of Dom Perignon. After dinner, their friends rolled up the rug and danced the night away. Don and I were exhausted from the trip and went to bed early, feeling and hearing the thumping of the music and laughter from below for hours.

The next day, we accompanied Lind to the fish market, where she bought the largest crab we'd ever seen. While JP was at work, lunch for the three of us was one gigantic scallop she cut out of its shell. JP also proudly fixed us the one dish he ever prepared, crunchy potatoes. He cut up and boiled potatoes, then threw them into a black iron skillet on high heat. He continuously added big scoops of butter until those potatoes were crispy and golden. For dessert on several nights, he proudly took a pear or another fruit and peeled the skin in one long spiral presenting it to one of us with a bow.

Don and JP got along famously, even with the language barrier. JP showed him their wine cave and was constantly bringing out his best wines, foie gras, and caviar to share. Sophie was ten and enjoyed trying out her English on us. I found her accent adorable. She was funny, energetic, and creative, and I loved having that chance to spend time with her. And all the while, we were treated like royalty. After dinner, while he was peeling an orange for me, I asked JP why he didn't come visit us in the States more often.

He replied, "Why would I need to visit the US again when France is the most wonderful country in the world, with the most delicious food, the best wines, and I have the most beautiful wife and daughter living here with me?"

I could see his point. I was also in love with France.

Our visit with them felt way too short. When we were leaving, JP hugged me and asked if we could join them on their vacation the next July to the Côte d'Azur. They were going to Grasse where they make perfume, to Nice, to Monaco, and into Italy. It sounded wonderful, and we were so flattered that they enjoyed us that much. But Don was thinking about buying a distributorship, and we wanted a baby, and it just didn't fit into our plans. I regretted that we couldn't make it work. I would have loved to spend more time getting to know my sister.

Don and I left Paris, taking the train to Bordeaux. We stayed the first night in the Terminus Hotel next to the train station. After dinner hosted by one of Don's wine suppliers, Don got an upset stomach. His discomfort didn't slow us down though. We had appointments and reservations made weeks in advance. We ate in two- and three-star restaurants and were hosted by various château owners. At Mouton Rothschild, we were included in a six-course lunch for the top chefs from Belgium. Baron Phillippe de Rothschild, our host, came out in what looked like his pajamas—Don said he always wore pajamas—and stood on a wine crate to welcome his guests. Poor Don, whose stomach remained upset for most of the tour, had to leave the table several times. He lost a lot of weight that trip. Not me!

When we left the Bordeaux area, we drove to Lyon to have dinner at Paul Bocuse's restaurant, a long-anticipated special treat. At a stoplight, another car ran into us. Neither Don nor I spoke French very well, but I hung on to the driver who had hit us while Don found a policeman.

We were upset about the incident and our damaged rental car, but we were more concerned about missing our meal. We made it just in time for our eight o'clock reservation, getting to meet both Paul Bocuse and his wife as they came around greeting their diners. The meal exceeded our expectations. As with most of our meals on this trip, there were many courses. But the one that stands out for us is the *Loup de Mer en croute* or seabass in puff pastry. The entire pastry was decorated to look like the fish, scales, face, eyes, and tail. It was gorgeous. The waiter very carefully peeled the pastry back and boned the fish and placed the pastry back on the fish. Not a bone remained in our servings, and it was delicious as well as beautiful. More courses followed. Then three carts of cheeses arrived. Don and I were shocked and embarrassed, realizing we had no idea what the cheeses were. So, we asked for help. The professional French waiter probably got a kick out of seeing the wide-eyed Americans as those three trolleys arrived.

Our eyes got even wider when three rolling carts of desserts showed up. Don chose the egg whites with caramel sauce. I had strawberries. After all of this we were offered coffee and cigars. The bill came to about $130.00. It seems like nothing now and wouldn't pay for one course with wine. Neither one of us will ever forget our dinner or the accident that might have caused us to miss it. The next day we called to tell Lind about everything, but she wasn't at home.

We left Lyon, drove two hours north through Burgundy, arriving in Beaune the day of a huge black-tie dinner at Clos Vougeot, a charity dinner and precursor for the charity auction at the Hospice de Beaune. We spent that morning with Andre Gagey, director of Maison Louis Jadot, who would be attending the dinner that night and had a christening for his granddaughter that afternoon.

We mentioned to him that he should make our visit brief, but he replied, "In Beaune we are never in a hurry." He then took us to one of their cellars housed in a 500-year-old monastery and spent a long time with us talking about and tasting his burgundies. The next day we visited the hospice, which was built in 1443 after the Hundred Years' War for the sick and poor. Now it is a historic monument with vineyards whose wines are auctioned each year. As we explored the gorgeous building we were imagining it filled with wealthy people purchasing expensive wines all for charity.

I must admit I was not a wine connoisseur. I was

drinking the best wines of France. All I knew was I liked this one or I didn't like that one. I had no idea how to describe them. Thank goodness Don did. He would try to tell me about the wines we would be tasting beforehand if he could. I was trying very hard to learn.

After Beaune, we drove into Alsace. I was dying to see stork nests, and Don wanted to meet a winemaker he knew from importing German and Alsatian wines. We showed up at the Trimbach Estate and spent an hour or so with the winemaker, Bernard Trimbach. Afterwards, he invited us to have dinner with him at his home. His wife, sister, and brother were there. They served us mushroom soup, cold cuts, salad, cheeses, and plum and blueberry tart for dessert. It was a lovely simple meal overlooking his beautiful vineyard.

We then drove to Strasbourg to catch a train to Trier and then a bus to Bernkastel, Germany, a wine-growing region on the Moselle River.

In my diary I wrote, "I spent three dollars trying to get into a toilet on the train. Instructions were in German. First, I didn't have the correct change. On the second try my money went down the sink, which was right outside the locked door. I went back to get more money from Don, then decided to just give up. He urged me to give it one more try. I did, and I was happy I did."

I continued, "Bernkastel is gorgeous." We stayed upstairs in a small inn, owned by a wine distributor Don knew, just a few feet from the Moselle River. That night in the small restaurant in the inn, his wife served us the best pork chops I have ever eaten, smothered in mushrooms, with great beer, and afterwards Don and I each had a huge cigar. We drank a lot of beer in Germany and smoked a lot of cigars, as well as tasting the best German wines.

After two nights, our host Ludwig drove us way up the

Moselle to the train station in Mainz. Don had spent four years in Germany and spoke the language very well. I could muddle through with French but did not know one word of German. We rented a car in Mainz, driving through Rothenburg to Dinkelsbühl, and stayed overnight in the Hänsel und Gretel Inn built in 1440. Then we drove to Ulm, where Don had lived. His German girlfriend worked in a shop there, and though he said he didn't want to see her we passed her shop more times than I could count. I believe he was hoping for just a peek.

We drove on to Füssen, which is one kilometer from the Austrian border and an easy trip to Neuschwanstein Castle. We walked all the way up from the car park. The castle was built by King Ludwig II in 1886 to withdraw from public life. He later died under suspicious circumstances. His castle is one of the most popular castles to visit in all of Europe.

Because we were so close to Oberammergau, we felt we just had to go there. Oberammergau is where the passion play is performed every ten years, but not the year we were there. Don's parents had attended the play when they were visiting him while he lived in Germany. The shops were packed with religious wood carvings copied from medieval originals, as well as carvings of drinking and hunting scenes.

Again, we called Lind but didn't get her. I wanted to tell her how great this trip was and how much we appreciated our time spent with them. I did send a few cards from several places to her and to Mom and Dad. I guessed I would just have to call when back in the States.

In Oberammergau, we saw a poster for a hotel that was having a wild game week. We followed the directions to the hotel and found we had to cross the border into Austria. The hotel was not in a town but situated on a glacier lake. The Alpenhotel Ammerwald was full, but we could make dinner reservations. We were told that just a mile farther was another hotel, closed, but the owner might let us stay, which he did. We spent the rest of the day walking the path around the lake. I took photos of the swans and a crazy German shepherd who kept jumping up and biting a knot that was on a tree. That night Don had rabbit and I ate *Hirsch*, or venison. We made reservations for dinner the next night, we liked it so much.

The next day we headed back over the border into Germany and rode a chuggy train up the Zugspitze, the highest peak in Germany at elevation 9,718 feet. I have a terrible time with heights and did not feel well when we got to the top. We took the cable car down, which was still scary for me, but faster, and that made it much better. We ate game again that night and the next day drove to Innsbruck, then the two-hour drive to Berchtesgaden and on to Salzburg. Driving through the Austrian Alps we could not help singing at the top of our lungs, "The hills are alive." We began our trip with many appointments on a tight schedule. Once we got through them, we were free to do as we wanted. I don't know if we will ever have another vacation where we will be quite so free.

When I look back on that visit to France, I realize it was the last best time I ever had being with Lind. We got along so well. I felt I was finally an adult in her eyes and not just her little sister. She and JP really liked Don, which made me happy. They seemed genuinely glad to have us there. But Don and I were bothered by how much she and JP smoked. I was also surprised by the scabs and rashes on JP's skin. Lind said his doctor told them it was caused by nerves. She said his job could be stressful and that he was easily agitated. Should I have seen these worries as bad signs for their future?

～ 16 ～

In the spring of 1978, John Davis turned twenty-one and my father—the grandfather John would never meet—had a stroke.

I got a call at work that Dad had been rushed to the hospital. His store manager found him in the warehouse of his office supply business, not breathing. When the medics arrived, they managed to resuscitate him and get him to Rowan Hospital, but his brain was damaged. He had been without oxygen too long.

At the hospital, the doctor told us that, inside his brain, an electrical storm with lightning strikes was going off every few seconds.

My brother and his wife Tass flew in from Cincinnati. Lind flew over from France. Since Sophie was in school, she stayed in France with her father, or probably with neighbor friends.

Dad had been in the hospital for twenty-four hours when the doctor asked for permission to take him off the oxygen machine. He said there was nothing more they could do and wanted us to be prepared for him to die. Mom was so upset and nervous that she left that decision up to Rick,

Lind, and me. We agreed with the doctor and felt it was the right thing to do. The doctor allowed us to come in while he was removing the breathing tube and shutting down the machine. We held hands and held our breath.

Dad didn't die. Unfortunately, for him and for Mom, he lived.

Mom blamed his stroke on her pestering him into building a new home near the Salisbury Country Club. His office supply business was a demanding one, and he should have retired earlier and gone fishing, or so she believed. My brother said Dad had not taken care of himself, eating too much fatty meat, drinking bourbon, and not exercising. I didn't think to blame it on anything at all. I just knew I was going to miss my dad.

Because Dad had been in the Navy during the Second World War, he qualified for treatment at Salisbury's large Veterans Administration Hospital not far from our house. Mom could not have cared for him at home, so we agreed to admitting him to the VA. Lind stayed in Salisbury for several weeks to be with her. Mother also had friends from her book club and her volunteer work with Meals on Wheels, as well as from St. Luke's Church, to keep her company. These wonderful ladies were her biggest support the next few years. I had a full-time job with a TV film company in Charlotte and could only be in Salisbury on the weekends. My brother now owned Cincinnati Fan and Ventilator and couldn't be away from work for long. We were all grateful Lind made the effort to stay for a while.

One day, while I was visiting, I was pretty sure I heard Mom say to Lind, "Wouldn't you like to find him?"

Lind didn't respond for a moment, and then I barely heard, "Mom, no. Not after all this time."

That was all they said. Because they spoke so quietly, I knew I wasn't meant to overhear. I was curious about the "find him" and the whispered secret, but I didn't ask. Why I didn't ask then, I do not know. I could have asked. I felt I could say or ask anything of Mom. Why didn't I bring it up with her later when she and I were alone? At the time I could only guess at what Mom was asking. I thought it could be about an old boyfriend of Lind's, someone Mom particularly liked.

Looking back, I wonder why the incident stuck so deeply in my mind. Maybe I was hurt at not being included in what seemed a secret between them. Did Mom and Lind discuss it further? I know now what that whispering might have been about. Mom might have been asking if Lind wanted to find her son. Why else hide it from me? Lind must have found Mom's question painful.

Personally, I would be curious to find out what had happened to a child of mine. But I am not Lind. I didn't go through the humiliation she suffered. I am even wondering how Mom could have asked her that. When she did, was Lind thinking, you forced me to give him up and now you want to find him?

John had a new life, and so did she. Yet maybe, from Mom's point of view, since Dad was no longer able to intervene it was time to try to reunite the family. Just more questions that I will never be able to answer. During the early months of Dad's stay at the VA, Mom, Don, and I, and a few of Dad's friends, would visit him even though he never showed any sign he recognized anyone. He was unable to move and had to have a special bed that rotated to help with his circulation. The visits became increasingly tough for Mom, and eventually she quit going. She had always proclaimed Dad the only love of her life. We understood why she couldn't face him being this way.

In September of 1978, Don and I had a blond, curly-headed son we named James Donivan, and nick-named him Justin. And I quit work. When Justin was about five months old, Don and I took him to visit Dad. I carried Justin in my arms and walked to the side of his bed.

"Daddy, this is our son, Justin, your grandson."

Dad looked at Justin and gave us the biggest smile, the first we had seen since his stroke. It broke my heart. A month later, March 28, 1979, Dad passed away. The church was packed for his funeral service. I took Justin's little shoe for Mom to hold during the service. Mom and I, especially, were going to miss having Dad in our lives.

The next summer, I talked Mom into renting a house at Wrightsville Beach so the family could be together. Lind flew over to join us. Lind's good friends from Chapel Hill were visiting their cottage on the Inland Waterway that week, so she excitedly asked me to accompany her to meet Jere and Marjorie Starling. Don stayed at the cottage with Justin and Mom.

The last time I'd been with Lind and her friends from Chapel Hill, I was twelve. I spent that time in awe of her and of Frank. This time, in 1980, it was as if I was watch-ing Lind from another place, a bystander not a sister. With the Starlings now, she seemed shy and a bit awkward. She laughed a lot, giggled. I could tell she was so happy to be with them, but she showed a nervous energy I hadn't seen before. My sister had always seemed so confident. She had been away for so long, living in a foreign country, married to a foreign man. Maybe she did feel awkward, out of place. Maybe she realized she missed what she'd once had. I sat there, part of the conversation but removed, too, just as I had been when I was twelve.

I watched Lind and tried to understand—not as her little sister but as an adult seeing the actions and reactions of another adult.

Jere Starling sent me an email and photos in 2012, when I began my search for clues to Lind's past.

> *Marjorie lives in Wilmington, NC, now. You may remember Lind was in our wedding in 1966. She and Jean Paul visited us in Louisville in '68 or '69, and Lind came to Louisville several years later. Marjorie and I were divorced in 1988. And in that year, I moved to Raleigh. Marjorie moved to Wilmington two years later.*
>
> *I am feeling sad that I don't have any anecdotes, scenarios, or stories to send you. I loved Lind. We saw each other mostly every day* [in Chapel Hill], *often ate together, sometimes went places together, did favors for each other, and sometimes just were. I think of her so often; she was one of the great happinesses I have known.*

Marjorie also emailed me:

> *She and I must have talked about not having a plan for "next." And we talked about "going West, Young Woman!" I went on and drove to Arizona—maybe she might join me—but she decided to go to France instead.*
>
> *She wrote letters to us for years, but in time I understood it was really Jere she was writing to—one of the "inner circle" at Clark Court. And it was Jere*

who opened and read her letters first, and I'm not
sure I always ended up reading them myself as time
went on...

I wondered if Lind's best friends were all men and if
there'd been more to some of those relationships. I wrote
Jere and asked if he and Lind dated. He replied:

No, Lind and I were not romantically involved. It
seemed from the beginning, we became very close
and dear friends, and we came to love each other
very much, but always as friends. I first knew Lind
soon after coming to Chapel Hill to graduate school.
She was living on Clark Court, Frank lived in a
communal house in Carrboro, and I lived in an
apartment on East Rosemary Street—then populat-
ed with large old houses mostly divided into student
apartments. Mine was directly behind the Raths-
keller Alley. I met her at a party at Frank's house,
then it went from there. I went to the University
of Edinburgh in June of '62. That same winter,
Frank was in Paris. When I came back, I moved
to Clark Court—my cottage was exactly like Lind's
but on the Church Street end of the row of three.
Frank lived on the other side of the street—and so it
remained until Lind went to Paris.
Marjorie was a senior when I arrived as a
graduate student. She majored in music, and we
both studied under Wilton Mason, who thought
we should meet. He assigned us both to play the
same piece. She went to Paris the following year
and met up with Lind. Then returned to CH in the
late summer before we were married the following

January of 1965. As you know, Lind came from Paris for the wedding. Then Lind married Jean Paul Coutou January 21, 1966.

Lind and Frank at a wedding party for Jere and Marjorie.

Lind, Sophie, and JP on a visit to Jere and Marjorie in Louisville, KY, several years later.

Lind smoking with Sophie in her lap.

— 17 —

When John followed me back to our house in Charlotte during his first visit in 2010, he asked to see anything of Lind's. I had saved the individual cardboard boxes Mom kept for each of us. John was fifty-two years old and had lived a full life, but the little boy who needed to know who he was and where he came from came to the surface. We pulled Lind's box out, and he spent much of the day planted at our dining room table, going through Lind's old photos, reading letters, and getting acquainted with his mother's past. At one point, he rushed into the kitchen holding one of Lind's high school yearbooks. He had discovered photos of Jim and Lind—the smoking gun, he exclaimed—proof his parents were at one time really in love. That meant a great deal to him.

Rick's daughters, Carolyn and Merrick, and their mom, Anne, lived close by in South Carolina. I urged them to come meet John that first weekend. My niece Merrick had recently visited Sophie in France and brought back a portrait of Lind painted by Clara Childs, a family friend from

Lind and Jim, from Lind's 1953 yearbook

Salisbury. Sophie pressed Merrick to bring the portrait back to the States, giving no real reason except it might be more safely stored there.

Soon after she was introduced to John, Merrick got up, went to her car, and retrieved the painting. She entered the kitchen, cleared her throat to get our attention, and pulled the portrait of Lind from behind her back.

"I wasn't sure what to do with this, thinking I'd save it for Sophie if she ever moved here. When Vaughan called and told me about you, John, I knew. The universe meant for me to bring this portrait back so that I could give to you."

We were all teary.

On Sunday, before John left, I looked for anything related to my sister that I might give him. I really liked John. He was my nephew, and I wanted him to have it all. I found children's books with her name scrawled inside and two high school yearbooks. In my bedroom was Lind's large wooden desk chair from high school. The initials "JR" were carved into the arm of that chair. I had always wondered about them and now knew they were Jim Rabon's initials. I gave the chair to John, and he was thrilled.

In July of 1980 after we returned from Wrightsville Beach, we had Justin christened at Christ Episcopal Church in Charlotte. We invited several friends back to the house, including his godparents, Mom, Lind, and a close friend of Don's and his wife from Germany. We ate outside on our big porch, and the weather couldn't have been nicer.

In Weddington, Don and I had a huge vegetable garden, made even more vigorous by the chicken coop that once stood in the same spot. We canned tomatoes and string beans, froze butterbeans, and made tons of zucchini bread. We cooked and ate corn the minute we picked it, becoming a "farm to table" household before it became a popular term. Don had grown up in Jacksonville, North Carolina, with a large garden, chickens, pigs, and a field of corn.

For lunch, Lind cut up a huge bowl of fruit and made tuna salad. Lind ate twelve ears of corn with a stick of butter, and nothing else. She said in France, hogs were fed the corn, it was not for humans, so she had missed it. During her stay, she indulged in other foods she loved, including bacon, cornbread, soft dinner rolls, and powdered donuts. We would be sure to send her a box filled with these items every Christmas.

After the christening we drove to Sawgrass, Florida, for a trip to Rick's condo. Don babysat Justin, playing in the pool and napping, while Mom, Lind, and I shopped and lunched. Even though Lind seemed tired and coughed more than I had noticed before, she acted happy to be with us, and we were certainly happy to be with her.

Mom and Lind during one of Lind's visit to the States.

— 18 —

I felt my sister could do anything she set her mind to. She had always been very creative, making beautiful suits, painting silk pillows, and stitching wall hangings she sold to Alderman Studios in High Point when she was in Chapel Hill. When her books were overflowing her bedroom in France, she got out her tools and built bookshelves in the upstairs hall, filling them with her classics, as well as novels that interested her like Jean Auel's *Earth's Children*, which we both loved.

She was also a terrific mom to Sophie, teaching her to sew and encouraging her to read great literature and listen to opera and jazz. I thought my sister was the most beautiful, intelligent, creative person I knew, and that Sophie was a lucky young lady to have her for a mother.

Lind created a charming home for them with a secret room for Sophie in an attic space off the second floor. She had a skylight added and carpeted the floor. Sophie had a small mattress to sleep on and an art table. She entered by pushing open a nearly invisible jib door. I loved Sophie's hideaway so much that I had one built behind a bookcase in our second son Gordon's room.

Lind converted an old shed in the side yard into a wonderful one-room stone cottage for guests, with kitchenette and bath. The interior was all white with pickled-wood floors and a white canvas curtain for the closet. When Don and I stayed there on a visit, she put an armful of tall white daisies into a white ceramic vase placed on the floor. Casement windows opened wide to the garden. I wanted to recreate that romantic shed back home too.

My sister's kitchen was a favorite. She collected miniature baskets and miniature tools. She loved hearts of all kinds—heart baskets, heart wooden bowls, stone hearts. She loved more primitive, less refined things, and she loved brown tones. She made wonderful funky tablecloths and napkins. Lind's kitchen was warm and cozy, the most pleasant place to linger, especially when she made fresh delicious soups—her watercress and potato soup was one of my favorites.

Lind would try out American food she loved on Sophie and JP, and even if they found it unusual, they had a good time tasting. She would make s'mores, burning the marshmallows on the stove. She grilled hamburgers on the terrace for Sophie's friends, and they would say they felt so American drinking Coca Cola out of Coca Cola glasses, while laughing with Sophie about her mom's American accent.

Lind would occasionally fix Sophie and JP fried chicken, which they would eat with their fingers. Rice was always Uncle Ben's. Sophie remembers most fondly her mother's biscuits—good ole southern biscuits—"with melting warm butter, salt, and sometimes honey," Sophie said to me. "Such a wonderful food memory."

JP was constantly showering Lind and Sophie with small gifts—and for Lind at Christmas and birthdays, beautiful coats and a diamond watch or earrings. He loved fine things and wanted them for his family. For years, at Christmas, he would send me his favorite perfume, Boucheron, which came in a bottle shaped like a large gold ring with blue glass on top, made to look like a gemstone.

Lind said nothing made JP happier than puttering in their yard on weekends, creating beautiful flower beds, and planting them with cutting flowers Lind could arrange inside. He mowed but never worried about weeds, saying, as long as they were green, no one could tell. While JP gardened, Lind and Sophie sunned on the patio and read. It seemed idyllic, perfect.

∼ 19 ∼

During his first visit with us in 2010, John mentioned an intuitive medium his wife knew of in Durham named Tomiko Omichi Smith. He said she was skilled at connecting with loved ones who had passed on, and John wondered about connecting with Lind. The idea intrigued me. For several weeks after that initial visit with John, I became more and more curious about Tomiko.

I have always believed there are people who are in touch with the spiritual, the universal, and are not bothered by the day-to-day busyness most of us have in our lives. These special people can see more clearly, have more intuition and empathy than the rest of us. I wanted to understand my sister better. With all I knew and was still learning, I felt like she was such a tragic figure. And I really missed her.

I finally got up the nerve to call Tomiko and set up an appointment. Over the phone, she briefed me on what she would need to channel the person or persons I wished to connect with.

"Please bring two blank sixty-minute cassette tapes, write on a piece of paper the first name of the person and their death date and bring that with you. That is all I will need."

I was anxious, but also could not wait to meet with her. When I arrived at her apartment, I calmed myself before knocking on her door, knowing I couldn't back out now.

A soft female voice with an accent answered, "Would you mind waiting just a few more minutes while I finish?"

"Of course," I said and walked back to sit in my car.

It wasn't long before a beautiful young woman came out of the apartment and smiled at me as she got in her car. She was pale and bald, but had a lovely, reassuring smile as if to say, you will be pleased you came—this will be good for you.

When she drove off, I walked back to the apartment and knocked again. A tiny woman, probably in her seventies, opened the door with a welcoming smile. Her small apartment was crammed with objects. It was filled with hangings, paintings, relics, totems, ankhs, fetishes, crosses, and candles. I loved it immediately. Books on religion, psychology, parapsychology, and the sciences were stacked on the floor, tables, and chairs. Her sitting area was cramped with a low worn beige sofa in front of a large double window. A wooden coffee table was in front of the sofa, and a straight-backed chair faced the table and the sofa. On the coffee table was a large boxy cassette recorder. I handed her the two tapes, and she inserted one into the recorder. She motioned me to sit on the sofa, and she sat in the chair across, facing me. Still nervous, I waited for her to speak, ensconced among all the objects and books.

"We will wait a few minutes in silence while I channel my mind to hear what is being said."

After a few minutes of quiet, she explained that she had been a part of The Psychical Research Foundation, but when the funding ran out and her husband died, she decided to continue her practice out of her home. She felt she was a "sensitive," not a medium or a psychic. She spoke about the many rooms of the future and how there were tasks to be done there and levels the deceased lived in. Then she said that she felt I was a priestess before I was born to this life. I told her an astrologer had said I was a waif, a beggar, living on the streets in my last life, and that was why I nested, why it was important to me to have a comfortable home.

"That was your earthly life," she responded. "You chose to come back a waif in that life to learn. You have had at least twelve lives before this one."

I wasn't sure I believed that, though I had been told before I was not a new soul. I really had my guard up, but both John and his wife believed in her, and I wanted to believe also. She looked at me quietly and smiled. Did she know what I was thinking?

"I will turn on the tape now," she said. "You give me the first name of the deceased person you want to know about and the date they died, and I will see if I can find them."

I asked first about my mom, who had died March 19,1996. Mom was my best friend, and I still missed her terribly. She paused for a long while, then nodded her head to indicate she found her. She spoke quietly and said that Mom seemed content and was happy that the situation had become easier for me lately. Which it had, so that made me curious for more. Then I said, "Gordon, March 28,1979." Tomiko told me my dad, who had been gone for so long, was happy among all his family. Nothing she said so far seemed extraordinary. I was a little disappointed.

Next, I mentioned Isabella, my grandmother known as Bam, December 30, 1969. Tomiko became more animated and said that she had moved away from the rest of her family and on to a much higher level. That threw me for a moment until I thought about what an amazingly strong, tough woman she was and how she had accomplished so many things in her ninety-one years of life.

I saved Lind for last. I hoped there would be something I could tell John about his mom. As nonchalantly as possible, I said Lind, December 26, 1998. Tomiko's eyes opened wide, then shut quickly, and she began rocking back and forth. She grinned like a Cheshire cat. Then her eyes opened again, and she looked at me directly.

"Your sister is very happy you have found him. She is also very proud of the way he has turned out. She is sorry she never met him on earth but is very glad that you know him."

"Know who?" I whispered.

"Her son."

I was dumbfounded. I hadn't told her Lind was my sister or that she had a son she gave up for adoption. I hadn't told her anything at all except Lind's first name and the date of her death. She didn't ask me if she was correct. She just turned off the tape recorder and rose, handing me the cassettes. She disappeared into a back room. In a few minutes, she returned carrying a small box.

"I was compelled to buy this yesterday, and at the time I wondered why. Now I know why."

She handed me a black, heart-shaped box that contained a crystal heart. Lind's favorite symbol.

"I think this gift must mean something to you. Am I correct?"

I hugged her and felt her warm and positive energy against me. "Yes, you are very correct." As soon as I got in the car, I called John. I was so excited, I was breathless. Several years later, I discovered an article about Tomiko's death written by Diane Brandon, a spiritual counselor. Tomiko had held master classes in the 1980s and Diane had attended. She wrote about how much Tomiko meant to her.

She said that Tomiko was a rare reader and spiritually advanced. Diane went on to say that Tomiko had a quiet dignity and strong moral integrity, that she appeared to be the essence of love.

When I remembered my meeting with Tomiko and our hug, Diane's observations seemed absolutely true.

～ 20 ～

In 1982, we received a call from Jean Paul. He immediately put a neighbor on the phone. "Lind has *problemes* with her *poumons*, lungs, and will be having a *traitement*, radiation. Jean Paul is very worried. Someone should come be with her."

Not sure if Lind had cancer or something else, Mom asked me to fly over to France immediately. I had a hard time leaving Justin, who was only four, but Mom had a horrible fear of flying and would have been panicked if she thought she had to go.

My sister, who started smoking in college, smoked unfiltered Gauloises cigarettes when she got to France. Frank, her longtime friend, told me later he had never seen a photo of Lind without a cigarette in her hand.

When I arrived in Paris, JP was very thankful, holding my hand and kissing me on both cheeks at the airport. I could tell by his expression that he was terribly concerned. When I got to the house, Lind was in her room. She said that they had found a little spot on her lungs, and it was nothing, but they wanted to do the radiation anyway. She didn't look like it was nothing. She looked tired and strained, and she was either very sick or there was something else wrong with her.

Lind's friends who visited downplayed her illness. I am sure they didn't want to scare her or Sophie or me. But I gathered from the few things JP did say, that she had been having breathing problems for a while.

"When we went to Africa several years ago, Lind tired easily and went to bed after dinner each night," he told me in broken English.

When he used the French word *emphyseme*, I was too naïve or scared to even contemplate the worst.

Tatyana was Lind's closest friend at the time. They met at a neighbor's home in Saint-Prix. Tatyana lived in Vienna, Austria, and ran a private kindergarten there. She traveled to Saint-Prix as soon as she could after hearing about Lind's illness. They both loved opera and would have long wonderful conversations—Tatyana sitting by the bed with Lind propped up on the pillows. Sophie felt that her father was a little jealous of the relationship they had. He felt Tatyana took Lind's attention away from him.

One morning a neighbor, Doris, who Sophie said was the wealthiest woman in their village and very *sympathique*, offered to take me to a Chanel fashion show. Lind insisted I should go. On the drive into Paris, Doris confided that she thought my sister and JP were not well-matched. She described JP as "like an old man, not exciting, very closed-minded, and old-fashioned in his thinking." Lind, on the other hand, she felt, was sophisticated, smart, and open-minded. Doris said she felt sorry for my sister. I wasn't sure how to respond, so I said nothing. She quickly changed the subject, but her observations were a warning shot for me.

Chanel, on Rue Cambon, wasn't far from where we had lunch, so we walked. I so enjoyed looking in the shop windows and staring at the beautiful French women with their petite bodies and shapely legs, shoulders wrapped in designer scarves. At the fashion show, thirty or so women, including us, sat in gilded French *bergère* chairs. It felt exclusive, obviously meant for the store's best customers. I realized this was a one-time event for me, so I savored every minute. On the way home, I gushed in English, relieved that Doris, who spoke English very well, could understand me.

When we got back, I wanted to tell Lind about my amazing time and thank her for making me go. I knocked softly on her door, afraid she might be napping. Hearing noise, but no response, I quietly opened the door. She was frantically stashing a cigarette in an ashtray under her bed.

"Lind. What are you doing? Are you smoking? Do you want to die?"

Her voice was shrill. "I don't care if I do!"

Then she burst into tears.

I wrapped her in a hug and started crying too.

"Lind! Oh god. I love you so much. You're not serious? What about Sophie? She needs you. I need you. There is so much to live for. You are the most creative beautiful person I know. How could you even say this?" Both of us sobbed as she poured out her heart to me.

"I am miserable. I married the wrong man. We have very little in common. He can be so critical of me. He has a way of making a face when he is unhappy with something I do or don't do. His expression makes me cringe. If the food is too cold or too hot or not his favorite, he makes that face. I can't stand to see it. He doesn't like opera and doesn't want me to go.

"He's too critical of Sophie. She's so creative and curious, but he is hard on her, expecting her to be more feminine, girly, like he imagined she would be."

"Oh Lind, I'm so sorry, but…"

Lind kept crying. "JP refuses to have anything to do with his side of the family. He thinks they are too bourgeois. Isn't that ironic? I am miserable, miserable. There is no way I can get away from this. I'm trapped. This isn't the life I thought I would have. I don't care if I die."

"Leave him," I told Lind. "Bring Sophie and come back to the States. You can stay with Mom until you find your own place."

But she went on to list the many reasons she couldn't leave. I tried to counter each one, but she countered back. Jean Paul, embarrassed by his first divorce, would be horrified by another. How could she live in the States, sick and with no money or health insurance? She couldn't take Sophie, JP's only child, away from him. For her, the only solution was to stay—even if miserable—and stay in the life she'd made for herself.

Of course, she could have come home. Mother and I would have helped her. Jean Paul would have been devastated but would have survived. Her leaving him might have saved two lives from sadness and depression—hers and Sophie's. But I couldn't convince her, and anyway, I still thought of her as my big sister, the intelligent one. This devastating conversation came fifteen years after she and JP had married and seventeen years before her long illness finally ended in death.

When I recounted this story to Frank later, he validated her feelings:

> I have the impression that [JP] even forbade her
> to go to the opera in Paris finally, even before her
> health got bad. I think he also made her get rid
> of her extensive record collection. By the way, I

*stopped smoking, cold turkey, the day I received her
letter saying she had emphysema, and I had been
smoking two packs of Gitanes a day. I still have
never smoked a cigarette since that day, February 7,
1982.*

Brigitte, her old roommate, also wrote me about that
time.

*As far as my impression of her marriage with J
Paul is concerned, I don't think she was very happy,
but of course we never really talked about it... One
very clear remembrance I have is of the day I went
to visit her when she was suffering from emphysema, and she told me she had sold all her records.
I realized then that she knew she was not going to
live much longer.*

After the treatments were over, Lind seemed to go on
as if she were cured and nothing had happened. She was
putting on a brave front—for a while anyway.

The year after I went to be with my sister, our second son,
Gordon Merrick Justice, was born in March of 1983. He
was a big baby, twelve pounds, three ounces, with a head
full of red hair. I told Don I was afraid to have another
child. What if it was even bigger? That was it for me.

～ 21 ～

In recent years, Sophie and I have talked about her child-hood and adolescence. I had followed her growth and progress through her mother's eyes. Not surprisingly, Sophie's memories were vivid.

Sophie recalled to me the wonderful times she had with her mom. From the age of seven or eight, she and Lind, in her camel-hair coat would take the train from the Ermont-Eubonne suburb to Saint-Lazare in Paris. Her mom held her hand as they walked to the Grand Opera House district. There was Brentano's bookshop, where they would spend hours looking for a special book for each of them. They would pause at Fauchon where Sophie pressed her nose to the window until they could stand it no longer and went in for a wonderful cookie or other treat. The stores Burberry, Old England, and Printemps were all close by. Occasionally, they would stop for lunch at the restaurant l'Artois, which faced JP's office, where Sophie would always ask for the meringue with strawberries and whipped cream, or lunch at Ladurée to drink tea with sugar and lemon and eat cucumber sandwiches and buy fondants candies that her mom would then put in her night table.

But Sophie also remembered from that same time, when Lind would leave Paris to come to the US or to visit her friend Tatyana in Austria, Sophie would be sent to a neighbor's home to stay. She would spend weeks with the Chabaneix, who also lived in Saint-Prix, or would travel with them to the Dordogne region on holiday. They had children her age, and she did have some good times, but she recently told me she felt abandoned and cast aside by her father. It seemed he could not cope with her.

When Sophie began to learn German at eleven or twelve, she and her mom would go on holidays to visit Tatyana in Vienna or stay with the Reyer family, who had a country house outside Vienna. They would attend music events and the opera with Tatyana and enjoy the outdoors with the Reyers. When it was snowing, they would all get into the sauna to get toasty warm, then run outside and jump in the ice-cold swimming pool. Sophie remembers that afterward they would sleep "like baby sheep."

In 1984, when Sophie was seventeen, she spent her August vacation before her last year of high school at a silk-painting workshop in the Alps. While there, she had an experience that upset her. When she returned home, she wanted to talk with her mother about it, but Lind, who we thought was doing better, was visiting us in the States. Sophie had no one to talk with—certainly not her dad. It would be hard for him to understand. She needed to talk with her mom. She could tell her anything. Not knowing what to do, Sophie left a note saying she was going to Vienna. She took the train to see Christian, a family friend she had a crush on. She hadn't told him or his family that she was coming.

Christian became concerned that Sophie's father didn't know where she was, so he called him. JP asked to speak with Sophie. Her father told her that her mother was back from the States now, wondering where her daughter was. He said Sophie should be ashamed for running off like that, that her mother was very sick, and she should not make her worry.

"All I felt was terrible guilt, that somehow I caused her illness."

Sophie immediately came home on the train and started her last year of high school. With so much worry about her mom, Sophie felt real fear and insecurity for the first time.

In 1985 after Sophie graduated high school from the Notre Dame de Bury, she saw a poster for a train trip to Peking, China. She convinced her parents to let her go. Three hundred and ninety-nine other young adults, ages sixteen to twenty, were also on the trip. Sophie had a marvelous time making many lifelong friends and wonderful memories.

From 1986 through 1989, Sophie was back in Vienna with her friends, working in a small theatre company, acting, making costumes, and painting scenery.

Home in 1989, and for the next two years, Sophie took courses on photography, literature, theater, and art history at the Louvre. Years later, she reflected on those years. She couldn't seem to settle into a direction for her life and seemed to be constantly sabotaging herself. If she found a good job, she would leave it. She would start courses and then not finish them. During this period I was out of touch with what was going on with Lind, Sophie, and JP. We had two sons. I was a freelance location scout for commercials, and Don had gotten a job with the Harris Teeter grocery chain as their wine buyer. I had no idea Sophie had decided to become a nurse.

She began nursing school in 1991 hoping to work with the Red Cross and travel. In the meantime, she took trips whenever she could. She flew to New Caledonia in the

South Pacific to visit a friend who was in her class. She stayed with friends in Beirut who were friends of friends from Syria who owned a coffee shop in Paris she frequented. Afterwards, Sophie came home to finish her written work and finals in nursing.

Then she was off again to work in a refugee camp in the Mali border in Mauritania, without even waiting to see if she had passed her exams. Which she had. She graduated in 1994.

It was obvious Sophie loved traveling and felt in her heart that she wanted to help people. I also wonder if she had an underlying need to escape. Her mom was tired a lot and coughing from incessant smoking, and her mother and father were not getting along that well. Even though Sophie was still being supported by her parents, she was also trying desperately to make a life of her own.

$$\sim 22 \sim$$

For the next several years, Don and I stayed busy raising our two boys and working. When Justin entered middle school, he changed from being a delightful young man—studious, smart, and fun-loving—into a brooding and unhappy son. By the ninth grade, we realized he was depressed, and the next few years were scary for us all. Gordon, caught between his parents and his big brother, acted as mediator—funny, loving, and desperately trying to keep everyone happy. By the time Gordon was a junior in high school, he was suffering too. Between work and difficult family life, I didn't have much time to keep up with how my sister was doing.

Her old friends from Chapel Hill stayed in touch, however. Frank sent her a photo of himself, Scott, and Norton together in Maine to cheer her up. They remained her dearest friends.

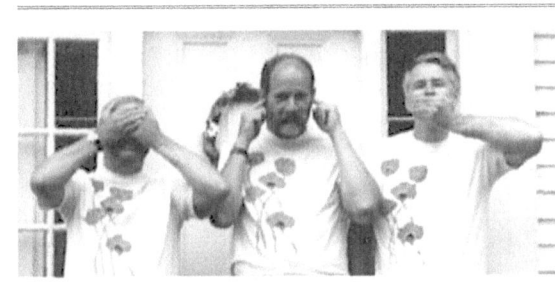

We were so wrapped up in our family, we didn't realize Lind was suffering more and more with emphysema and that it might actually kill her. And as Lind suffered, so did Sophie and JP. They had to sell their home in Saint-Prix because it exhausted Lind to walk up the stairs to her bedroom. They moved to a small apartment building in the town of Ermont that had an elevator to their second floor.

If dying was a way for Lind to escape life, then she chose the most horrible slow death of all. Not being able to catch her breath, not able to travel, ride a bike, or even walk up the stairs would be terrible. Did she still feel guilt from all those years ago? That was a question I did not know to ask at the time.

In 1993, we moved into Charlotte from Weddington. Our sons were in school at Country Day, and with traffic on Providence Road increasing, the drive into the city from our home was becoming horrendous. Mom was happy we were in town in a nice neighborhood, and it made her drive from Salisbury to visit much easier too. As an added benefit, we were close enough to the boys' school that they could walk.

Just a few years later, in March of 1996, Mom died from a heart attack. Her housekeeper called me at work to tell me Mom wasn't feeling well and that she would get back to me if it turned out to be serious. But before I could get to Salisbury, Mom was gone. My biggest regret will always be not arriving in time. Mom had been in good health and then she was gone. Mother was giving, funny, loving, and kind. The male nurse with her at the hospital told me her last words to him were, "You are an angel."

Lind, too sick to fly without oxygen, couldn't come for Mom's funeral. I missed having her there. If it weren't for a friend of Mom's who helped me with funeral plans, I wouldn't have had a clue what to do. Rick, retired now and living in Fort Lauderdale, drove up from Florida to attend the funeral and so we could meet with the lawyer about Mom's will. I called my sister several times to go over the details. Too exhausted to talk, she basically just listened.

In the early stage of her emphysema, Lind used oxygen only at night or when she took a nap. As time went on, she rested more and more often. Soon, she used oxygen waking, resting, and sleeping. Speaking became a struggle, her breathing raspy and conversation exhausting. When we talked on the telephone, which wasn't often, the call had to be brief. Then the calls from her stopped. When friends asked to visit, she refused to see them.

JP, who was twelve years older than Lind, had also been a smoker, but he told me he quit when Lind had her radiation treatments. It eventually became difficult for JP to look after Lind. Sophie was living in a one-room flat in Paris— virtually a large closet with a door and window. She visited her parents as much as she could to help, while working nights for a private agency, distributing blankets and coffee to the homeless living in the streets of Paris.

Frank later recounted in a letter:

I always saw Lind when I was in Paris. Sometimes she would come into Paris to meet me. (I remember once we met at the Café de la Paix for coffee and sat outside facing the Paris opera.) I also visited Lind and Jean Paul a couple of times when they lived in Saint-Prix, and once or twice in Ermont, always for just an hour or two. By the time I saw her in Ermont, she had emphysema badly enough to have a long tube attached to an oxygen tank. But she

always made the best of it, and I never heard her
complain.

"Mom did not talk much toward the end," Sophie told
me. "When she did, she mixed languages, using a lot of English words and confusing them for French. And then she
stopped talking at all. I missed my mother's voice so much. I
would speak to her, but she no longer could answer, though
she would nod her head and smile."

Lind's doctor eventually admitted her to a hospital for
lung ailments. The large sanitorium was built sometime in
the 1800s. It was far from Paris and isolated.

Sophie said it was "decayed like the patients inside. That
depressing place was for people with lung sickness, a place
you are sent to die. And I suppose Mother knew that when
she was sent there."

"Near the end when I was with her, I could tell she
struggled very hard to say something. I had to put my face
right up to hers to hear her. She whispered, 'I love you, Sophie.' That was the last thing she ever said."

On December 26, 1998, my sister died at the age of six-
ty-one, just two years after our mom died.

Don and I flew over for my sister's funeral in January '99.
I was confused when JP and Sophie met us at the airport
and immediately drove miles out into the countryside. As
we rounded a corner, Sophie turned to Don and me and gri-
maced. "Voilà," she said, pointing to a looming, foreboding
hulk of a penitentiary-like building. I felt sick. My sister's
life had ended there? My beautiful, smart, talented sister?

JP pulled the car up to the left side of the horrible structure and parked. The place felt deserted, silent, no birds
or humans in sight. JP checked several doors, apparently
looking for someone, while Don, Sophie, and I waited by

the car. I noticed the building had bars on all the lower basement windows. Beyond a fence stood a massive tree with bark ripped from the trunk and, under the tree, several large animal footprints.

"Wild boars," Don said. "I guess that's why they have this fence. You wouldn't want them roaming around in this parking lot."

Jean Paul continued to knock on doors until one finally opened. He waved us over, and a small man in a dark suit held the door for us. He then led us down several steps. Below ground now, the tiny, rectangular, barred windows near the ceiling let in the only light in the long, dim hall. Everything felt gray and dark—the horrible dingy building, the overcast sky outside, wild boars in the silent woods, and the musty hall in which the four of us walked single file. We followed the man into a room where a body lay covered on a gurney. The room had an unpleasant smell; Lind had been dead for more than two weeks.

I stood horrified as the man pulled back the sheet and revealed Lind's gray, sunken face. I didn't want to remember her this way. Jean Paul and Sophie kissed her. I knew I should, too, but I just couldn't. They both looked at me; I looked down. The man in the black suit covered her face again and spoke to JP in French I did not understand.

Another man entered, and they rolled my sister out of the room. We returned to the car and drove around front, where a black hearse waited. We followed the limousine carrying Lind's body down the long drive and onto the winding roads back to Paris. When I looked back, I was relieved to see that looming gray building disappear behind us.

The four of us didn't have much to say during the long ride back to town. I thought about how long my sister had suffered, and how hard it must have been on Sophie and Jean Paul. Lind had been stoic, not revealing to me what she was going through. Yet, in retrospect, I could see the clues. Lind had called often after Sophie was born and in the early years of her daughter's life, then stopped. She'd written long, newsy letters every week or two, then those arrived less often, and finally stopped altogether. Her tearful statement years ago when I was with her for the radiation treatment finally came true. What a miserable way to go. It is hard for me to think about the years she spent getting sicker, willing herself to die, I guess.

As we drove into Paris, Sophie told me she'd moved home to help with her mom before the doctor sent Lind away. When she bathed her, she had noticed cuts on her wrists.

"Poor Mom was so miserable, she wanted to die," Sophie said. "But she couldn't go through with killing herself. Although it looked like she tried many times."

"Sophie, how awful. Poor Lind." That's all I could bring myself to say.

But whenever I think of my sister, the thought of her so desperate and miserable that she would cut herself, and many times, haunts me.

The limousine entered a park-like setting through ornate wrought-iron gates. The crematorium, a long, low, curved structure, stood in the center of the park. Rows of columns fronted it and held the sloping roof overhang. A small group of friends had gathered. Tatyana, Lind's best friend from Vienna, was there. I regret now that I didn't know how special she was to Lind. If I had, I would have tried to talk with her more. Sophie said that after her mom was so sick, Tatyana would visit often and sit by her mom's bed all afternoon reading to her or telling her interesting stories.

Brigitte was there too. She had been Lind's roommate, the person Frank suggested Lind meet on her initial trip to Paris. Jennifer, British and remarried, had traveled from the Dordogne region of France to attend. She, her husband, and children had lived in Saint-Prix when Lind and JP did. Theirs was the family Sophie stayed with many times and traveled with on vacations. Lind had stood up for Jennifer in court through a messy divorce from her French husband. A male friend of Sophie's was there, an older man, poet, and pipe smoker. He had been an emotional rock for her through her ups and downs during her mother's illness and her own depression. Jean Paul's boss also came, along with several others. These people had been her good friends in France and yet were strangers to me. I didn't think about that then, but I think about it now. I could have talked with them, asked them about themselves and about my sister.

Lind's closest male friends from Chapel Hill hadn't been able to make it. Frank lived in Boston, where he'd retired from teaching. Scott, recently married for the second time, lived in the Languedoc region of France, far from Paris. He was also retired, having taught in Edinburgh, Scotland. Norton, a Rhodes Scholar, on the board of trustees of the North Carolina School of Science and Math in Durham in 1979, and a director of the South African Education and Environmental Project, lived in South Africa with his wife. Neither Jere Starling nor his ex-wife, Marjorie Crane Starling, both of whom lived in North Carolina, were able to make the trip.

Our small, quiet group was led into a massive marble room. A few folding chairs had been placed facing eighteen-foot-tall bronze doors carved with gigantic leaping flames. As I sat, looking at those intimidating doors, my mind raced, and I began to create a movie scene in my head—a scene about what I expected might happen next.

I imagined my sister's body on the gurney would be rolled slowly past by four pale, solemn men in conservative black suits. The massive bronze doors would sound like thunder as they rolled open, and flames would be revealed, leaping skyward from a fiery furnace somewhere below.

The hall of mourners, dressed in blacks and grays, would gasp, horrified, realizing what was about to occur in front of them. The pale solemn pallbearers would lift Lind's frail, lifeless body and gently slide her off the end of the gurney and into the scorching pit. My beautiful and gifted big sister would become ash. A few minutes later, we would hear faint vibrations of music as her soul released from her body to rise and be greeted by other souls in the universe. Then a collective sigh, and Lind would finally be at peace.

Slowly, the massive doors would rumble shut as the pallbearers quietly rolled away the gurney, and all of us— her family, her friends—would relax, knowing the worst was over.

When the furnace cooled, a silent workman who controlled the flames from below would carefully shovel her ashes into an urn to be presented to Sophie and Jean Paul to carry home and put in a sacred place.

Back to reality, I looked around. Everyone had taken their seats and was waiting for something to happen. Three young Russian street singers Sophie had met in Saint Petersburg walked to the front and sang several beautiful a cappella ballads. Jean Paul cried uncontrollably. Sophie held his hand and wiped his face with his white embroidered handkerchief.

There were no flowers. When I asked Sophie why, she said her mom had requested none, though my sister loved flowers.

There was no religious service. No minister or rabbi or Buddhist priest offered encouraging words about life and death. Because Lind was agnostic, she had wanted none of that either, Sophie said. Did Lind think she didn't deserve it? Did she feel she wasn't good enough? Or was Lind so worn out from life that, in the end, she just didn't care?

There was no eulogy. Not one of us stood to say even a few words about Lind—nothing of her creativity, intelligence, charm, laughter, smile, or having been a loving mother, caring wife, wonderful friend.

The singers finished and walked out, the service over. The room returned to quiet, except for JP's sobbing. Lind's body had never entered the room, the bronze doors had never opened, and there had been no leaping flames or fiery furnace. I was stunned. Lind deserved my movie version. She should have had a glorious finish and a magnificent send off. I wanted her soul to rise out of that fire, like the phoenix in the story I have always loved. I wanted my sister to be carried to a beautiful place, a place of peace and love, where emotional or physical pain didn't exist. I wanted so badly to see her ashes rise high into the heavens or be carried away on the wind. I wanted my big sister to have the dramatic finish I felt she deserved.

Still, the room was quiet. Did the others wait, like me, for something more—for those doors to dramatically open, for a eulogy, for a prayer? Sophie and JP finally got up, and then everyone else followed.

We stood outside under the columned roof and waited as it started to drizzle. Friends hugged us and drifted away to their cars. An hour or more passed before the urn was handed to Sophie. Inside that urn was her mother, my sister, Jean Paul's wife, my parents' beloved oldest daughter.

And inside that urn was forty-one-year-old John's birth mother. It would be eleven more years before John was able to find us.

That summer, Sophie visited and brought the urn with her. Sophie; Don; our two sons, Justin and Gordon; and I drove to Salisbury to have our own brief ceremony at Dad's and Mom's gravesite. First, we stopped in front of the little white house with the big white columns where Lind, my brother Rick, and I grew up. It looked so tiny. How could I have played Putt-Putt in that front yard? Then we drove out Innes Street, past the Dairy Queen and under the concrete railroad bridge—two of the many Salisbury landmarks I loved.

We reached Memorial Park by late afternoon, as the sun set and shadows deepened. I hadn't been there since Mom's death in 1996, and it took a few minutes to find our family markers.

"We love you, Mom," Sophie said. "And want you to be close to Roz and Big Gordon." Then she threw a handful of ashes into the air and passed the urn to me.

"I miss you, Lind, and only wish I had been able to spend more time with you."

Then Don, "We love you, Lind."

"I didn't know you very well but always liked you," our twenty-one-year-old son Justin offered.

Gordon, then sixteen, threw his handful of ashes over our heads and shouted, "Have fun in heaven."

We all scooped up more of her ashes, releasing them to the sky as we twirled and sang special songs Mom had

Sophie with her mother's ashes next to Mom and Dad's gravestones.

sung to me and then to our sons—"I See the Moon and the Moon Sees Me," "Day Is Done," and "Baby's Boat a Silver Moon." Our mother had also sung these to Lind and Rick, and Lind had sung them to Sophie. Sophie laughed—we all did—as the sun disappeared below the horizon and a train whistle blew in the distance.

— 23 —

As I worked on this story, I emailed John, asking if there was more he had learned from his visits with his birth father. I wanted to know a bit more about their relationship. John emailed this:

My dad Jim was a hard-working, good-looking football player, who was a class ahead of Lind in high school. In the afternoons he worked construction at the VA hospital. At night he worked in the police department.

When Jim graduated, he went into the army and served two years as a medic. Jim was drafted for the military football team, so he got to play football while in the service.

After Jim graduated from Catawba College, he went to work for an international company. He married on August 27, 1961, and he and his wife Carol lived in Germany for a time, but later returned to Salisbury and opened their jewelry store in 1984.

Finally, when Jim was contacted that the laws had changed and that I wanted to meet him, he was in his early seventies. By then he had given up thinking he would ever get to meet me.

My dad, Jim, is quiet, good, and kind, but finds it hard to talk about all those years of pain. He is happy he knows me, my wife, and our children though, and it is wonderful for us to get to know him, his wife, and grown children. We do spend as much time as we can with them.

When I was put up for adoption, the Children's Home told my future adoptive parents that there were two other couples who were interested. Your mom and dad had asked that the adoptive parents be Episcopalian, educated, and located in North Carolina. My adoptive dad, Johnny, was an Episcopalian minister. A mentor of his happened to be associated with the Adoption Home Society and took a special interest in me. Johnny and his wife Sarah were chosen to be my parents. I then became John William Sutphin Davis, Jr., son of Rev. Johnny and Sarah Davis.

He also said that when he was about six years old, Sarah and Johnny explained to him he was adopted, just as his sister was. I know they sat him down and presented that information in the very best way they knew how. Yet I am also sure he wondered why his birth parents would give him up. Anyone would wonder that, especially a young child. Was there something wrong with him?

He said that after learning he was adopted, he went through a short insecure period. He hid under tables in the classroom and had problems reading. But his teacher told his parents that he was so smart and not to worry. Johnny and Sarah thought he was just adjusting to this new information and felt his confusion would pass. However, they did find him someone to talk with.

> *I remember that the psychiatrist was very kind and did make me feel better. As I grew into a teenager, several people told my parents that I looked like a Kennedy. They knew I was born in Washington, DC, so it became a running joke with my parents and their friends that that was who I was. I did try to find out more about my birth, but it seemed to be off-limits to me, so I gave up asking.*

Johnny and Sarah Davis served in several North Carolina churches over the years. In addition to St. Stephen's, they served Christ Church in Rocky Mount, the Church of the Holy Innocents in Henderson, and the chapel at St. Mary's College in Raleigh—an interesting coincidence for me. After retiring from the ministry, Johnny taught science and math at Vance Academy in Henderson. Later he and Sarah moved to Richmond, where their adopted daughter lived. John and his family lived nearby. After Sarah's death at age eighty-six in May 2010, Johnny moved in with John's family and lived with them until his death in 2012.

John had started the process of finding his birth family in late 2009 and decided not to tell Sarah. She was frail at the time, and it just seemed too difficult. After Sarah died, John did tell his adoptive father that he had found his birth father, Jim, and his mother's family. Johnny was thrilled for John, offering to investigate John's genealogy for fun. His adoptive father also got the chance to meet John's birth father in the summer of 2010. John, his wife, his kids, and Johnny were at Figure Eight Island, outside Wilmington. Jim and his wife drove up from their cottage in Myrtle Beach to Figure Eight for a visit.

— 24 —

Though Sophie and I didn't talk often after her mom's death, when we did, our telephone conversations were long and personal. She felt, I believe, I was her surrogate mother. For many years, Sophie suffered bouts of depression, which she said were caused by her mom's illness, as well as her father's disappointment in her. Yet Sophie had an energetic spirit I adored. She was vulnerable and curious and, when happy, would skip and dance and hug everyone around her. Then the dark side would appear, and she'd stay in bed for weeks. I tried to help but could do little from five thousand miles away. I fretted about her smoking and encouraged her to exercise. She listened, agreed, and said she would try.

I believe Sophie's salvation is her curiosity, a trait she doubtless inherited from Lind. By the time Lind died, Sophie had traveled extensively; she seemed to thrive on immersing herself in other cultures. She could speak a bit of Russian, German, Spanish, and was pretty fluent in English, thanks to her mom.

At one point, Sophie traveled to Colombia, where she stayed with friends who were involved in helping to maintain and record the lifestyle and language of indigenous people there. This trip left a deep impression, and Sophie became curious, she told me, about American Indians.

That gave me an opportunity to lure Sophie back for another long visit in the US. JP bought her an airline ticket, gave her some money, and on September 1, 2001, she flew from Paris to Charlotte. A week later we found ourselves in Albuquerque, Santa Fe, and then Taos, New Mexico. I happened to have a good Charlotte friend, Jo Cross, whose daughter was a lawyer and professor of Indian studies at the University of Montana. Jo and her daughter had recently taken pottery classes in New Mexico with a woman from the Taos Indian tribe, and Jo agreed to come on this trip with us as our tour guide.

The Taos Indian's pueblo, or village, was built sometime between 1000 and 1450 AD and is believed to be one of the oldest continuously inhabited communities existing in North America. In the writings about Taos history, it is said they migrated from the Four Corners region—the southwestern corner of Colorado, southeastern corner of Utah, northeastern corner of Arizona, and northwestern corner of New Mexico—because of a long drought. The Taos Indians have, for centuries, enforced a strict policy that forbids marriage outside the pueblo. They also have a long-standing tradition of secrecy around their sacred beliefs and customs, so they have long been self-isolated from modern influences. At the time of our visit, approximately 150 people lived in the village full-time with about 2,600 living on the 100,00-acre reservation. No outsider is allowed to step foot on their sacred land, which is part of the Sangre de Cristo Range. Tourists can only visit unrestricted parts of the pueblo village for a fee.

The Taos reservation includes the sacred Blue Lake or Ba Whyea, which had been taken by Teddy Roosevelt in

1906 for federal parkland then given back by President Nixon. The Indians believe getting their lake back was the most important event in their recent history, since they believe the Blue Lake is the place of their creation.

We flew to Albuquerque and drove west to the Acoma Pueblo, the "village of the strong people" who had built homes in the side of the rocky mountain. Then we headed to Santa Fe for a few days. I'd attended a photography workshop there and was excited to go gallery and museum hopping. My favorite, the International Folk Art Museum, surely would have been my sister's too. Lind loved naïve art and primitive tools and furniture. JP preferred gilded French furniture, which made their home interesting and diverse in its style.

My friend Jo had collected western Indian pottery for decades and knew all the names of the famous potters, sculptors, museums, and ceremonies. We couldn't have been in better hands. Jo had found a little cottage in Santa Fe we rented for a few days. We enjoyed music in the square and perused the local merchant's wares, their jewelry and crafts displayed on blankets in the shade of the adobe buildings. Sophie took it all in, rejoicing in her new experiences.

One morning we drove twenty miles north to a place called "Where the Water Cuts Through," the San Ildefonso Pueblo. We arrived in Ildefonso Pueblo on September 10 and joined the locals in celebrating the ritual of the Corn Dance, which is said to go back beyond time to the myths of origin when supernatural beings, men, and animals lived together with their Earth Mothers, Blue Corn Woman, and White Corn Maiden, beneath the Lake of Emergence. The ritual consists of many dances and costume changes, representing the corn as it is given to man and slowly grows into food for the people.

I had never had more than a passing interest in this culture, yet I found myself impressed and moved by the story of the Corn Dance. The trip was beginning to turn into a spiritual journey, something I had never anticipated happening.

On the drive back to Santa Fe, Sophie couldn't stop talking and smiling. Seeing the traditional dance and costumes of the American Indian was exactly what she had wanted. She expressed sadness her mom couldn't experience this with her and hoped she watched us from heaven or some other wonderful anxiety-free place. She said her dream for her life now was to move to the American west and have a little land for a garden and a donkey. Then she would be happy.

The next day was the birthday of Jeri Track, one of the potters from the Taos Pueblo who Jo and her daughter knew. Jo had invited Jeri and some of her family for lunch. Jeri, who was turning eighty-four, had modeled for many of the books and articles written about the Taos Indians. Her daughter, Soge Track, a writer and potter, would bring her own daughter, Dakota Star Concha, and infant grandson, Jack. An aunt, Juanita, also planned to join us. Jo said Juanita was well-known for her storyteller dolls of Indian mythology and had married a famous sculptor whose work was in the Millicent Rogers Museum in Taos.

Jo told us these Pueblo women were sophisticated, educated, creative, and highly respected leaders in their tribe. In the Taos Pueblo—unlike most pueblos—Taos women have equal status with the men.

The morning of September 11, the day of the birthday lunch, Sophie was just getting out of the shower, I was putting on makeup, and Jo was wrapping a present for Jeri when the telephone rang.

It was Soge. "Do you think you will still want to take us to lunch today?"

"Of course," Jo answered. "Why? What's wrong, Soge?"

"Turn on the television. The news isn't good."

"Vaughan, please turn on the television," Jo said to me.

"Oh my god," I gasped when I realized what I was seeing.

"Is this real?" Jo questioned.

"What is it?" Sophie asked.

"Soge, I will call you back in a few minutes." Jo put down the telephone.

The three of us sat on the bed and watched as a plane flew into one of the Twin Towers in New York. Then another. We sat stunned, viewing the disaster over and over. Sophie was shocked such a horrible thing could happen in America. We all had mixed emotions of fear and confusion. Would this happen again? Would they, whoever they were, strike the White House, Atlanta, Charlotte? Would we go to war? Who could hate us so much they would do this?

As time for our lunch date approached, we agreed we couldn't watch or listen to the news any longer. We finished packing to move to Taos, and Jo called Soge to let her know we were on the way.

The drive to Taos and Orlando's Cafe was solemn, but I felt some sense of relief as we joined the already present Taos ladies. Jo introduced us, and we gathered at a table on the patio. The vast countryside around us was quiet, peaceful—a world away from New York. The small restaurant had only a few other patrons, and no televisions.

"See the sky." Juanita pointed, and we all looked up. "There are no spider threads. Spider Woman has stopped weaving her web."

She was right. No planes flew, so no vapor trails. The sky was pale blue, silent, and eerie. Sophie and I were determined to make the most of our time, so we asked the women about their lives, their families, and what they were currently creating. I liked being in their company. They seemed so calm, wise, at peace. After all, they belonged to a tribe that had survived severe mistreatment and upheavals yet had never gone to battle.

I commented on what a good baby Soge's grandchild was, and she explained how the tightly wrapped papoose carrier made babies feel secure. At that moment, I wanted to be young again; cocooned in a papoose; unaware, like baby Jack was, of the dangers and terror in our world. I felt it was a blessing that Mom and Lind were not around to experience this horror.

We ordered the avocado pie, at the Taos ladies' urging, and all had seconds. I wanted thirds but restrained myself.

With no planes flying for several days, we knew we'd miss our flight home, so when Soge asked about our plans, we agreed we had none.

"If you must stay a few more days anyway, why don't you come to my home on the reservation, and I will help you make a small, wood-fired clay bowl," Soge offered.

"We would love that," we agreed.

The next morning, we had breakfast on the town square of Taos before heading to Soge's. Other diners were as somber as we were, talking in whispers about what they had seen on the news or read in the paper.

After breakfast, we headed north of Taos, following the map Soge had drawn for us. We arrived to find Soge piling branches in a bare spot in her yard away from the house and trees. She lived in a small, cinderblock house on Pueblo land outside the pueblo itself. Jeri, Dakota, and her baby lived with her, yet her husband, Dakota's father, lived in a house inside the pueblo. A curious arrangement, but we asked no questions.

Dakota played with Jack at the picnic table. We settled in on benches on either side. Sophie, intrigued with every little detail, seemed as happy as I'd ever seen her, which made me happy. In my mind I told Lind I was glad we had made this trip for Sophie and wished so much she was with us, still alive, away from France and her pain. As Soge dipped water out of a small gulley with a coffee can, she explained how she had dug the gulley to divert water from a nearby stream. Water was scarce and sacred in the desert, and, on the reservation, never wasted.

Soge had already dug the clay for our bowls and placed it in four mounds on the table. The clay, full of mica, sparkled in the morning light. Sophie loved the sparkles and painted her lids with the mica clay, commenting on her new "eye shadow." As she batted her eyes back at us, I wished her mom could have seen how happy she was.

Soge instructed us to dip our hands in the coffee can of water and start working the clay to form a ball. Once we had a round ball, we could smooth and shape our bowl, pushing our thumbs down into the center of the ball. The bowl, when finished, would be small and simple, yet it held such significance for the Taos tribe, she said. A bowl could hold water, be used to cook food or to gather things from the garden. I admit I felt guilty about the way I lived—all the stuff I had, the way I took things for granted. Making money was important, it bought stuff. But I could see I had missed out on an essential way of living and seeing. It reaffirmed my feeling that we were sharing a kind of spiritual journey.

Throughout the morning, we worked on our pots, smoothing the clay with our fingers. Sophie, Jo, and I sat at the old picnic table under a large cottonwood tree, at peace and having quiet conversations with the three Track women. Soge's daughter took her baby out of the papoose and bounced him on her knee. Dakota had been born deaf, but she had learned to dance, sing, and make small, beaded dresses and mica pots. The horrors of New York felt far away, unreal.

When Soge inspected our bowls and pronounced them finished, we squeezed water out of the leftover clay and back into the coffee can, which Soge poured back into her gully. I looked at Jo and Sophie and could see how happy and content we were to be in this place. I wished Lind had had such a place of contentment. Maybe hers was the little house on Clark Court, or holding her little girl Sophie, the patio in Saint-Prix, or the nights at the opera.

We stayed most of the day under that tree, eating, laughing, talking. On the ride back to the adobe hotel, we agreed this day was a gift. We had spent time in the world of Mother Earth and Animal Spirits. Not one of the three of us wanted to leave that place, or for that feeling to end.

It was several days before we were able to book a rental car for the drive home. On the trip east on I-40 we met so many people trying to get home too, all of us shocked and worried about what had happened on September 11—and what the repercussions of the attacks might mean.

～ 25 ～

Even though Sophie's creativity, insatiable curiosity, and love of learning were similar to her mom's, physically she was French—dark hair, brown eyes, a small frame, and bushy brows. Yet, as she grew older, I told her she had our grandmother Isabella's nose, my mom's complexion, her mother's figure. It always made her happy to hear she had physical traits from our side of the family.

Her dad often made unfortunate and tactless statements to Sophie—that she looked older than her cousins who were the same age, that he wished she was more feminine like her mother, that she had no idea how to take care of herself. He helped support her financially her entire life feeling she had no idea how to handle money. JP loved her, I know, and didn't realize how hurtful those comments were to young Sophie, who was grasping to find out who she was, why her mother was so sick, and why she felt so insecure and restless.

My husband thought the world of JP, making the case that he went out of his way to be nice to us on our visit to France. All of that was true, but I believe JP was out of his element when it came to being the father Sophie needed.

From an older generation and more provincial lifestyle, with no hobbies and not many outside interests, except for his weekly card game with neighbor ladies, JP wanted to be the man of the house, looked up to, listened to, probably even obeyed.

An American wife, especially one like Lind who had suffered pain and embarrassment and became more independent because of it, didn't always see things his way. Yet once Lind became sick, it seems she lost that spirit of independence and gave up. What happened to the sister who had stripped down to her underwear and jumped in the river, who had gone off to live in France away from family and friends?

Sophie's father died on November 5, 2004, six years after Lind. He was seventy-seven. Sophie was thirty-seven, ten years younger than the brother she did not yet know existed.

When JP was too ill to be alone, Sophie went to live in his apartment with him. Her nursing degree was a great bonus. In 2001, she had started working at Centre de Retention near La Defense, where she assisted doctors with health checks for undocumented migrants before they were sent to trial. She also worked part-time dispensing medications at the jail. Now that her father was gone, she would be totally alone. Even though JP had some family still alive, none of them were very close with him or with her. So, of course, I flew over to be with my niece for her dad's funeral. I took our younger son, Gordon, then twenty-one, with me.

Sophie made all the arrangements, so her father's funeral was even lower key and simpler than her mother's had been.

A few of JP's relatives who I had never met came back with us to the apartment, where Sophie, Gordon, and I were staying. Sophie opened her dad's best wine and sherry and served *pâté*, dates, and figs. Sophie's uncles and aunts strolled around surveying the seven small rooms. Sophie accompanied them, offering them furniture they especially liked—typical of Sophie, so generous, never wanting to come across as greedy. I wanted to stop her, tell her to think about it first. This little bit of furniture, part of both her parents' lives, was all she had left. But I said nothing. She gave it, and they took it. The entire time they were there picking out Sophie's furniture, I wondered if these were the family members that JP talked about—the ones he was not so fond of.

When everyone left, Sophie turned off the heat and threw open the windows in the living room, in spite of the freezing November chill. Wrapping herself in a wool blanket, she told us she needed fresh air to breathe. As Gordon and I sat miserable in the cold, I wondered if she was worried about how to pay for the heat or if she just felt the need to shiver in her sadness. Now she was by herself—both parents dead. What would her life hold when there wasn't anything to hold on to?

For most of the four days we spent with Sophie, she lay on the sofa, with her rolling papers and what she called *tabac* nearby, as she talked about her mom and dad. She confessed being afraid she'd never have a healthy relationship with a man, questioned her sexuality, and chastised Gordon for his laziness. Sophie told us she was not happy with her jobs and wished she didn't have to work at all. I wasn't sure what to do, knowing her mom would have been distressed to see Sophie this way, depressed and alone. Gordon and I tried to encourage her—telling her that she was able to do anything she wanted now. She had friends all over the world—Beirut, Africa, Austria, Russia, South America—who she could visit.

"We would love to have you come stay with us for a while, Sophie," I suggested. She continued rolling her cigarette with no verbal response.

One of the nights, a sweet older couple in the apartment complex invited the three of us for soup and dessert. It was a welcome relief from the sadness pervading the apartment and, for Gordon and me, a blessing to be in a warm room for even a little while.

One of the days, Marjan, who had been a good friend to my sister, took Gordon and me to visit Auvers-sur-Oise just north of Paris. Van Gogh moved there to be near his brother in May of 1890, after spending a year at an asylum in Saint-Rémy. He painted seventy-seven of his best loved paintings in the three months before he committed suicide in July.

The charming little village was almost exactly like it had been when he lived there. We had a wonderful time walking around, going to the old church and cemetery, visiting the tiny room where Van Gogh slept. Marjan knew a lot of the history and was a wonderful tour guide. Still, Van Gogh's depression made me think of my sister and Sophie and the very dark times in their lives.

My spirits were lifted when we drove to the Musée de l'Orangerie Paris to see eight paintings of Monet's water lilies, known as *Les Nymphea* series. Natural light on the paintings from a skylight in the ceiling gave them a special glow. In one oval room, four paintings show the reflections of the sky and vegetation in the water from morning to evening. In the second oval room, the paintings showed contrasts created by branches of weeping willow around the water's edge. The paintings were huge, breathtaking, enveloping the entire room. I was so blown away and wishing that my sister and niece were here with us. Maybe this beauty would have lifted Sophie's spirits a bit too.

Marjan then took us to her home and made a late lunch of cold cuts and bread, before returning us to Sophie. Lind had mentioned to me the first time I had visited Paris for Sophie's baptism that people in France could be standoffish and it took them a while to warm up to you or to let you in their lives. But that day, Marjan, whom I had never met, spent the entire day with us, speaking fluent English. She didn't have to—no one had asked her to entertain us—but she did. Overwhelmed by her kindness, I will always remember and be grateful to her for the day of art and history.

On our last night in France, Sophie wanted to go to one of her and her father's favorite restaurants. She had recently gotten her driver's license and was excited about being the chauffeur. The night was misty and foggy, the roads curvy and hilly. Sophie sat far up in the seat, her face jutting over the steering wheel so she could see the road. Gordon and I were amused and, at the same time, anxious about her driving.

"Well, I just learned it, you know," she said.

"We can tell," Gordon answered wryly.

The front window on her side kept fogging, and I had to keep wiping it off so Sophie could see. Gordon sat nervously in the back seat. After my hundredth attempt to keep the fog off the windshield, Sophie and I looked at each other and burst out laughing.

"Oh, of course," I laughed.

"What?" Gordon leaned forward.

"Sophie is leaning so far forward over the steering wheel to see the road that her breath is making the windshield fog!"

Sophie's mood was changed, and we giggled and laughed the rest of the way. The restaurant up on a hill was an old greenhouse, all glass on the sides and roof. Seated in this room, we were above the mists hanging in the valley below. We could barely see lights twinkling in the village windows. Dinner was fun, and the food was delicious and a good note on which to end a sad, poignant visit. Gordon and I flew back to Charlotte the next day. I worried about my niece now alone and too many miles away.

When asked for memories of Lind, Jennifer de Chabaneix, her British friend from Saint-Prix now living in
Dordogne, wrote:

> Lind was the most elegant lady. She'd go off and
> visit something in Paris with heels and beautiful
> clothes. Even at home, she was dressed in lovely
> clothes, had the figure of a young girl, so slim. She
> was an excellent gourmet cook—she had to be, I
> suppose, with Jean Paul—and always put me to
> shame. I still have some of her recipes. She drank
> vast amounts of very weak tea all day long, par-
> ticularly in the latter years. She had this passion
> for opera, and when we saw Werther at Covent
> Garden, London, she wept like a child through the
> rather grim story!
>
> She had a great sense of humour and was a sin-
> cere and loving friend to me; she even gave evidence
> in my favour to the judge in my divorce, and I will
> never forget this. I saw her in the hospital before I
> went to England, and she was in a really bad way.

*When I got back, I stayed with my son Nicholas in
Saint-Prix in order to go to Lind's funeral. (It was
an awful ordeal, I thought.)*

*I hear intermittently from Sophie. I hope she
keeps up with her American heritage. It is such a
great gift to have two nationalities.*

My love to you, Vaughan,
Jenny

The year after her father's death, Sophie sold most of
the remaining furniture from her parents' apartment, keeping a few of her mother's favorite pieces—an antique collection of salesman's miniature wooden tools; an extensive
naïf Christmas village, each piece collected over many years;
and Mogrador, the large Japanese sculpture Lind purchased from Max Steele, the professor and author, paying
in installments.

I love my sister for choosing this root carving and for all
the other wonderful and unusual items she collected. I love
that she had such a curious and wonderful intellect. I wish
she would come back for a few minutes, so I could let her
know how much I wish I had been her friend, not just her
little sister. I would have learned so many things about literature, music, and art, and I am sure, I would have become
a more interesting person.

Sophie soldiered on, finding a house in the country near
Saint-Pons de Thomieres in the Languedoc-Rousillon region. It wasn't her little plot of land out west with the Indians—she wasn't ready to stray that far from home—but it
was her first step of real independence, a baby step but an
important one. True to her generous nature, after paying

too much money for the house and plot of land, she allowed the previous owner to stay until she found another
place to live, while Sophie had to stay with friends.

Lind's close friend from Chapel Hill, Scott Griffith,
lived less that a kilometer from Sophie's new home—even
closer if you go by foot through a meadow. He wrote me,
describing the cluster of three small hamlets.

> *Leaving the town of Courniou—on a road that is
> going up a valley, you come to the first of the three
> hamlets … Usclats le Bas (the lowest). That's where
> I live. Further up is the second of the three Usclats,
> called Usclats du Millieu—the middle Usclats—
> that's where Sophie lives. Further on is the last
> Usclats, Usclats le Haut—the highest. As you go up,
> the hamlets grow smaller. Le Bas is the largest. Le
> Haut is the smallest with only two or three families
> in residents. Most homes are stone, like mine, and
> are reasonably large for France and quite old. Mine
> dates from the 17th century. There are many out-
> buildings of all sizes, an ancient lavoir or washhouse,
> and an ancient communal oven. Trees are numerous,
> chestnut, walnut, ash, cypress, and there are gardens,
> large and small. Near my house is an orchard which
> produces plums, apples, and pears. There is a natural
> spring which never dries and feeds the washhouse
> and many of the gardens. It is a very calm place.
> Though during the hunting season—deer, wild boars,
> birds—it can get noisy with dogs barking, guns firing,
> and hunters shouting, but only on weekends and
> Wednesdays and only for three or so months a year.*

Sophie's new home, about two hundred and fifty years old, needed a lot of work. Originally, farm animals lived on the first floor, the family on the middle floor, and hay was stored on the third floor. The house had a large stone shed and, across the narrow dirt road, lots of land for a garden. I still worried about her. Even though she held good jobs off and on, she had never made enough to support herself entirely, so her father had pitched in.

At this point, she didn't quite understand the value of things or how to handle her small inheritance. In her naïvety and generous spirit, she had recently given sixty thousand euros to a friend to build a home in Africa. She hadn't realized that she would eventually need that money to live on herself.

Sophie's nursing degree turned out to be a godsend, not just for her livelihood, but for the shut-ins in the rural villages around her. She soon had a job with a government-supported team of nurses who traveled the area, helping bathe the elderly, giving them shots, and checking on their general health and welfare. She told me how interesting the countryside in her area was to drive, so different from Paris. Up the mountain, it snowed, then back down, sunny, and warm. She seemed fascinated by the elevation's effect on weather and how it changed in such a short distance. I pictured her leaning way over the steering wheel, as she had that night she drove us to a restaurant, looking through the windshield, smiling in amazement at the world around her.

Sophie worked alone but occasionally joined the other women nurses. Scott and his wife had her for dinner from time to time. Scott told her he would always be available should she have an emergency. He had loved Lind as a dear friend, and now was a friend and protector for her daughter. At home, Sophie had cats for company and got to know her neighbors.

Then she met a man named David and became infatuated, eventually inviting him to live with her. David did odd jobs and bartered, hoping to pay off debts from a job that failed. He was living in his truck with his dog, Hera. He was tall and thin, the physical type of man Sophie was attracted to.

David proved a wonderful help in the garden and was very handy as a carpenter. Sophie loved that he was creative—growing indigo and dying clothes. He was very motivated, something she couldn't always muster.

Still, Sophie had very dark days, or weeks, when she hardly functioned. Over time she felt David was becoming too critical. She might have an idea for something they could do and he would immediately say it wouldn't work. His attitude toward her could make her question herself and made her angry. She praised him for the work he did, but she felt she never received praise in return. Neither was good at expressing what they truly thought. Many times she thought of asking David to move out and told me so, but they hung on, each needing something from the other. I was glad she at least wasn't alone.

Several years passed without us communicating much, which wasn't unusual. Neither of us liked to talk on the telephone, nor were we letter writers. And Sophie hated and avoided the computer, which would have been the easiest and best way to stay in touch.

I heard David and Sophie had gone to Morocco, where David had hired a family to weave carpets he designed. In 2009, Sophie returned to France, but David stayed behind. Once the carpets were finished, he would bring them back to France, and he and Sophie would sell them at weekend markets in nearby villages. He also had a loom in the house and had learned to weave some of the simpler carpets himself. Sophie helped dye the wool from plant leaves and berries she harvested in the area. That part of the relationship was good.

But the emotional side had not improved. Sophie still seriously considered asking David to leave. But she didn't want to be alone. Insecurity plagued her, and sadness and fear seemed overwhelming. She felt paralyzed.

It was around this time that I called Sophie with the joyful news that she had a brother. John was fifty-three. Sophie was forty-two.

"I have a brother?"

"Yes, Sophie. Your mom gave him up for adoption when she was nineteen."

"Why didn't she keep him?"

"Well, it was the 1950s, she was young, and I think our dad made her give him up since she wasn't married. At the time, it was an embarrassment to the family, though it wouldn't be as shocking now. In that time nice girls didn't have sex, and if they did, the babies were usually given up and given away. Sophie, he seems really nice. I'll meet him soon, and I'll tell you all about him. He's coming for a weekend."

"I have a brother," she repeated. "A real brother."

With that one phone call, Sophie later told me she felt a bit stronger, a bit braver. She said just knowing she had a brother somehow gave her enough strength to sit David down and tell him how she felt, what she needed from him. And if he left her, well, she had a brother.

David didn't leave. He opened up to her instead. He told her things about himself he'd never told anyone, things that happened to him in his childhood that made him feel insecure. He promised to be more supportive, to trust in her judgment, and to trust in her love for him. Dark clouds slowly lifted for the first time since losing both her parents. Sophie had a brother.

Still, three years passed before she was ready to meet John—three really long years to the rest of us who were so ready for them to meet.

Jennifer de Chabaneix's 2012 letter continues:

> I am amazed about Lind's son and the wonderful effect it is having on Sophie and you. She needs so much love, that child. I had a card from her from Morocco mentioning David. It is a pity Lind did not confide in me as I too had (what was known at the time as) an illegitimate child when I was 17 and I too gave it up for adoption and have never traced him, nor him me, and the doubt always persists about who he is, what he is, etc., etc. It is not the sort of thing one talked about, and many women live their secrets all their lives.
>
> Nowadays with the pill and disjointed families—people would laugh!

～ 27 ～

Having a brother changed Sophie's feelings about communicating by email. She and John began emailing back and forth, sometimes sharing the emails with me.

In December 2009, Sophie addressed an email to "johnny james brother!"

ça alors !

john you have a french sister!

Mom, or Rosalind, but her mom also, so ours was called Lind, grandmother was called Roz. Mom loved opera, so after university in Chapel Hill, she bought tickets for Bayreuth festival in Germany, as going stopped in Paris, stayed, met my father & became both nationalities.

we will send you pictures, and paintings! she was handsome, witty, curious of people & anecdotes, big reader & music listener, it seems your daughters have inherited her elegant spirit.

would you mail your post address?

please trust me when I tell you I am very happy to meet/know/discover you

ça alors!
much hugs to all around (do you live w. garden
&/or animals?)
welcome in france!

Sophie's next email was a short one, but with so much feeling.

You can't imagine how much I've been missing you,
big brother, since I was born.

In the next, she wrote:

Wind has woke up during the night, and rain ac-
companies. I hear both in the linden tree in front of
the kitchen door, as well as a Schubert piano/violin
beautiful piece offered by the France-musique radio
station night program, as well as the dog girl Hera's
snoring!
*   On a stool in front of me, licking her beautiful*
self, girl cat Misty. She's the one who mysteriously
appeared in the mist of November as I came back
from a two months journey in Morocco and decided
to stop working as a nurse. First phone call at home
was from Vaughan telling me about you folks!
*   So, Misty is a special cat.*

I love reading emails from Sophie. Her writing is poetic. She is a wonderful observer of nature, which is very precious to her. She may not write often, but each email is written from her heart.

John wrote me in the winter of 2010:

Vaughan,
    I got this from Sophie this morning. The photo shows a cool old stone wall I guess is in her back yard. She was complaining about the "pylon de electric" near her house. It is one of those high-tension 72,000-volt transmission towers. I thought she was talking about a telephone pole.
    Hug yourself for me.
    John
    PS She sounds so wonderfully, refreshingly eccentric in a great way. I hope I meet her someday.

Sophie wrote to me:

Sweetest! Need to know more about Big Gordon [Sophie's name for my dad], his own parents & stories ... 'cause now I'm angry at him! Would you help me in understanding? Maybe your own thoughts, too? I still feel packed in other's will, not strong enough to untie the threads & I keep falling over those threads!
    Morning coffee huuuuuuuugs!

I totally understand Sophie's confusion and anger as she tried to make sense of her parents not letting her know that she had a brother somewhere out there. She felt anger toward our parents for making Lind give up her son and felt hurt her own mother never told her. I felt all those things too, but maybe not as strongly as she did. My feelings were sadness and loss for Mom, Dad, and my sister because they would never know John.

From Sophie to John:

frère john!
    *Cold & snow ... David rehabilitating rabbit
house, but today too icy to work outside, hot bath &
nap, that's a winter occupation! I cooked yesterday
my hamlet's new year cake. Dried fruits & nuts
(brandied for two neighbors, not for the two others!)
& will visit this afternoon. Listening to Mercedes
Sosa, Argentinian, I think, discovered her thanks to
friends as I stayed few months in Bogota, Colum-
bia. Working with street children & prostitutes in
the old town center, living nearby in a little house
w. patio. There learnt Spanish, told to be the purest
because old Castilian. Also came back with more ki-
los corresponding to "arepas"—corn pancakes—hot
chocolate & queso!*
    Sophie

From Sophie to me:

Sweetestyoudulidu,
    *Package has been sent, w. mostly books, cd, little
frame & pictures for brotherjohn*

From me to John:

John,
    *This is very emotional learning things and trying
to understand things...*
    *The emails from Frank, Scott, and Norton make
me cry every time I think of them ... just think of
them. I want to take Lind in my arms and hug her*

sooooo hard.

*Mom would be so thrilled to know you! I am so
sad that she didn't have a chance to … But, somehow I feel Mom and Lind are involved in all of this
and happy we are now all together.*

Xo

Vaughan

From John to me:

*I believe someone (or more) is up there steering us
all through this and making it happen. I am blown
away every time I think about it. Here's to us mor-
tals in an attempt in understanding Lind's wonderful life (and pain) in the small way we can. Huggs,
very soon.*

From Sophie to John:

morning hellos

*Interrupted yesterday by electricity break, often
happens when strong winds … I should say breaks,
cause it happened a dozen times in the day! So yesterday rice, the almost last tomatoes, fried w. lots of
garlic around 11, that's my brunch time … waking
up, it's black coffee with cigarette … then made a
dough for a strawberry pie for David, with "crème
patissiere"—eggs, milk, sugar, flour & vanilla—
which he loves! Then drove to the neighbour hamlet
at the Raynaud's house to be with Edmond, 97
years old, strong health but forgetful, as his daughter Suzanne went to a reunion. I keep him every
Monday, each time they go to the opera in Toulouse*

where they have a subscription, and when she needs. This pays the monthly bills.

From Sophie to me:

!you are our family knot!
Dreaming of crossing the Atlantic Ocean with our little house-truck & driving around. Montana could be a great visit. I'll send you myosotis seeds I collected yesterday on the blue pot from the picture, may You & John put them on Mom's heart [for Lind's gravestone]?
more hugs than alphabet combinations!

Sophie to me, September 2011:

I love you and miss you & and you know what? I miss my mom Lind so much some days...I suppose its universal mother & child. As I feed Marie-Helene, the neighbour's cats, news on, showing the beginning of 9 11 ceremony how not cry upon men's foolishness?

John to me, November 2011:

I am worried that Sophie is quickly marching down the same path as Lind in terms of her smoking....I don't want to offend her, but we all love her and want her to be around for a long time and be heathy. Think about it...Lind was 61 when she died and was sick for 10 years. Sophie is 44 and if she follows Lind's path, she has only 8 more years to be healthy before she starts to get sick. It rips your

heart out when you think about it in those terms.
  Love and hugggs all around,
  John

I know how John felt. I had been worried about Sophie's smoking for a long time. I would think she would be afraid after watching her mother suffer and knowing that it killed her. We talked about it. But Sophie didn't seem afraid and it obviously was a crutch for her.

Even now, I continue to hope living in the fresh mountain air of the South of France will keep her hanging on for a long time for us.

Sophie to me, November 14, 2011:

with sweet hairy Misty cat on the lap, 1st morning hot coffee in the guts, I think of you! neither need Misty or coffee for doing so of course, but it's a picture of awaking me.
  Ok-yes, I forgot the cig, still no self-portrait w. no cig…

John to me, February 2012:

I got approval to place a marker stone [for Lind] in the Earle space [in Salisbury].

Sophie to me and John, March 10, 2012:

I've been searching for flights w. Scott
  Yeeeeeeeeeeeeeeeeeeees, I'm afraid but slowly over come it! September October definitely is better, fairs & markets, garden works being lighter.

Barbara [Scott's wife] *tells that in July the prices go lower, the exact reservations I'll do in the summer.*

I love u & miss u soooo. you I know my eyes are soak wet just thinking of hugging Vaughan at the airport…what will it be with you John, will be needing rehydration, is your tap water sane?

Oh la la

sun shining, days grow longer, today wash will hang outside, ending drying by the fire.

From Sophie to John, March 21, 2012:

Sorry I am not coming, September is a holy month for me, apart from equinox, Mom & Dad were both born in September it's also a beautiful song, written by Kurt Weill, sung by his wife Lotte Lenya.

From Scott Griffith to me, June 2012:

I see Sophie all the time, usually at the Wednesday market in nearby Saint-Pons, and each time I give her a big hug. Her man, David, has a stall at that market usually, selling artisanal Moroccan fabrics, carpets, woven jackets, and hats, loverly things. We got a wonderfully colourful dining room carpet from him last year. Everyone covets it.

She's dying to meet her new stepbrother. Proudly tells us his news often. Was very taken, for example, to learn that he ate bread made with Kamut, I think it was. We had a look at airline booking sites with her a while back when she was studying a trip to your family reunion earlier this year. Hope that went well.

I'll give Sophie your hug day after tomorrow. As aye, Scott.

Sophie to me, September 16, 2012:

sweetest, all I will be able to give this coming thanksgiving is my skypeface...
finance at the underbottom of the well, we have to dig & work more our "Main des Sables" [the website created to sell David's carpets].
I'm so sorry
I call you this afternoon my time & hug you til then or later

Sophie to me, November 2, 2012:

sweetest!
when are you gathering at your home? may be possible to organize a skype meeting? many xmas markets & fairs, but hopefully I can manage the computer anywhere?!!!
as to xmas present for me, know what I miss sometimes? a little corn pipe, I remember bringing one back & I really enjoyed puffing it until I gave it away...
and the face jugs are the only objet filling my overfull house!
Pottery still is a big pleasure to use & admire, I suppose you can keep food in them? or more likely liquids? [These items were all purchased when Sophie came to the States for a visit.]
David has gone to gather chestnuts. I at last open the kitchen door & enjoy green sounds &

smells, w. Misty cat on my lap & cold coffee at
handreach.
Chlorophylianhuuuuuuuuuuuuuugs!!

Emails came irregularly, but they came for three years.
We had a Skype call with Sophie over Thanksgiving in
2012, when we celebrated a big family get-together at our
house with John and his family; my brother, Rick, and his
daughters and two grandchildren; as well as Anne Earle,
my brother's first wife and his girls' mother.

And then a hint of a reunion from Sophie to John,
March 2013:

good morning Brother!
    are you ready to meet me this year? I think I am,
at last! it's decided, I come over, for a short time,
essential to meet & talk & hug
    no, donno when, sometime in the summer, as my
work slows down a bit may be?
    materialy speaking, I still need your family fi-
nancial help I'm afraid, hope I'll be worth it!
    please prepare a drawer of handkerchiefs, I
already got wet eyes just thinking of this trip, I'm an
emotion bundle!
    Love you sooooooo
    your little sister

April 2013

bonjour Brother!
    would mid-July be good? With my job concerns,
it's the soonest & most convenient time. Your own
existence filled up the infinite devilish black hole I

had. I needed 3 years to digest the parameter of a brother 10 years older than me, 53 years hidden to the family, 43 years hidden to me, 61 years hidden in our mother's sorrow.

your letter to Vaughan telling who you are & the wish to know us has helped me find my place on earth. You are the brother I've been searching for all over the planet backstages, running from Paris to Peking & Nouméa & Bogota & Saint-Petersburg, from the nursing school to the jail, old people home & maternity hospital down to the guts of urbanity with street children & prostitutes & homeless.

I eventually may begin a normal family & friends life and develop a sense of happiness & creativity. You already filled my soul, Brother John! I humbly hope I may help filling yours. Hugs to all around, your little French sister.

From John to Sophie:

Sophie,
We look forward to your coming sooooo much. You will fill a hole in my soul. Let's set a date early so the airfare will be more reasonable. We are all doing well. I work all the time.

Then, finally, confirmation arrived for John and Sophie's highly anticipated reunion:

To Vaughan:
To brother John:
Here I come on the 10th of July at 14:25 your time, US airways

Charlotte, and go back on 22nd at 16:50
I still can't believe what I say as I say I go &
meet my brother!!!!!!!!!!
Now I have the ticket, it slooooooooowly becomes
concrete and I get Excited all shaking inside!
Hugs so much on you all

From John to Sophie:

We are so looking forward to your trip. As you
pack, please bring a couple of swimsuits. We are
going to spend a few days at the coast. You might
want to get a new one over here.
Much love,
John

Sophie replied:

Great idea, salt sea and sand, long time I've not
seen the Atlantic! Nobody ought to laugh as I wear
my old-fashioned but so comfortable swimming suit!
Let me tell you the diet I follow … if I don't,
I fall sick and I'm very bad mooded! This I don't
want! strictly vegetarian and organic (some rare
obligatory exception!) Implying eating much grains,
seeds, beans, & of course fresh fruits & veggies. I'm
used to cooking all those, and it won't be a bother
I hope. I propose I drive to the supermarket with
Vaughan as I arrive, this might ease your thoughts
about it, and mine!
Oh dear all! Can't believe it!
Huuuuuuuuuuuuuuuuuuuuuuuuuuuuuuuuuuugs

After reading Sophie's email about her food needs—and not wanting her to be "bad mooded"—I had a ready supply of lentils, oatmeal, broccoli, asparagus, fresh fruit, nuts, dates, and beans. Of course, Don and I eat like this most of the time anyway—sort of. The afternoon Sophie landed in Charlotte, Don made his hearth bread just for her.

Sophie's plane arrived on time, but customs seemed to be especially hard on dual citizens that day. It took an hour and a half for her to appear, rolling a cart of bags, filled mostly with presents for everyone. I am not sure I had ever been this excited. Sophie would soon meet her brother, and John would soon meet his sister, a part of the family he had always wanted to know and be with. My heart felt so big, I thought it would explode.

John and I had planned Sophie's schedule in advance, a packed one! She'd stay with Don and me until Saturday, when we would all meet in Salisbury for a memorial for Lind. After the service, everyone would return to our house for a cookout. On Sunday, John, his daughter and son, would drive Sophie to Figure Eight Island to spend a few days at

Don and Sophie that first night of her trip to meet her brother.

the beach with his wife and oldest daughter. Then they'd return to their house in Virginia, and I'd go up Thursday and bring Sophie back to Charlotte on Saturday, giving her Sunday to rest and pack before flying out Monday.

Sophie seemed pleased we had all the healthy foods she mentioned in her email. She asked me to take photos of our meals so she could show Scott and his wife when she returned. Sophie wanted Scott to know her American family didn't eat junky food like the Americans they read about.

Sophie admitted to being excited but nervous about meeting John and his family. Planning a few days with us on the front end proved fortunate, since she slept most of the day following her arrival. Exhausted, anxious, and dealing with menstrual pain, she experienced a brutal first couple of days. But by Friday, Sophie was feeling better, and Saturday turned out to be a perfect day.

We arranged to meet at a restaurant in Salisbury first, and arrived early, making small talk and constantly looking out the window. Sophie, jumpy, suggested we go sit in the car, saying it would be easier to see them drive in. A little frazzled myself, I agreed. Finally, John's big black Cherokee drove into the parking lot and parked two spaces away.

"There they are, Sophie. He's here."

John got out of the car, and Sophie leapt from the back seat and ran to him with her arms open wide. John picked her up and twirled her around as she cried, "Brother, my brother!"

It is hard to describe what an emotional moment this was for all of us. We talked, hugged, and cried until Sophie jumped in John's car for the short ride to College Barbeque, where we were to meet Rick's family—Rick and Cassandra, his current wife; Anne, my brother's first wife; and daughters Carolyn, and Merrick plus Carolyn's children Jack and Rozzie.

Carolyn, Jack, Merrick, and Rozzie squeezed into a large corner booth while the rest of us pushed two tables together nearby so no one would miss a word. Our excited energy filled the small restaurant already packed with diners. In spite of Sophie's strict vegetarian eating rules, she ordered barbeque that day.

After a lunch with everyone talking at once, we piled back in our cars. Sophie sat next to her brother John in the front seat of his car as they headed for the cemetery. Once there, we swarmed the plot near the bell tower where my parents and paternal grandparents were buried. Already in place in the very center of the other markers was Lind's pink marble heart stone. Our family—on earth and in heaven—surrounded her with love.

The inscription read,

In loving memory of Rosalind Earle Coutou
B9/19/37 D12/26/98
Given by her children
John William Sutphin Davis, Jr.
Sophie Jeanne Coutou-Earle

"l'essentiel est invisible pour les yeux
on ne voit bien qu'avec le Coeur"

The French expression is a quote from Saint-Exupery's *Le Petit Prince*, or *The Little Prince*. It was one of Lind and Sophie's favorite books. Sophie suggested it to John to have engraved on Lind's gravestone. The translation is mine: *The essential is invisible to the eyes. We see well only with our heart.*

We grew quiet, then John read what he had worked on the previous night.

> *Dear God in Heaven, we gather here today to re-member Lind with this memorial stone at our feet. We pray and are thankful that she is in spirit with her parents and grandparents. We pray that she knows that Sophie and I have found each other. I pray that she knows her sacrifice of me at my birth was not in vain.*
>
> *I pray that she sees the person I have become and sees herself in me. I pray that my mother knows that I have always loved her and had her locked in my heart in the most sacred space.*
>
> *Lord, I know my mother still loves us who are still here on earth. I ask you that you might listen to her fervent prayers for us. Help me to grow into a new and deeper relationship with my mother now, as I long for the day when we will both meet in your embrace—freed from all that might have hindered our lives together on earth, knowing and under-standing everything we did not know or understand during this lifetime.*

*I ask you this with faith in the resurrection,
trusting my mother's love, and desiring that she
knows my love for her. Amen.*

Then his youngest daughter read a prayer written by her
mom:

Dearest Lind,

*I know your beautiful spirit is surrounding your
family, especially on this day, as they honor and
remember your life on this earth.*

*I feel your presence constantly as I know you
watch over your children and grandchildren. I
know your beautiful spirit lives on in John and
Sophie, and our children, John William, Liza, and
Grace.*

*I sincerely thank you, Lind, for bringing John
and Sophie into this world. I so wish I could have
also met and loved you in this lifetime.*

*I promise you I will look after John and the kids.
And I will try to get Sophie to quit smoking and to
come visit all the time!*

*Finally, Lind, I want to honor you and your
life and know that you are always in our hearts,
thoughts, and prayers.*

*For everything there is a season
and a time for every matter under heaven;
A time to be born and a time to die;
A time to break down and a time to build up;
A time to weep and a time to laugh ;
And a time to love, which is now;
May we all walk in God's love and light
and be well.*

There was not a dry eye in the group. I knew that would happen, so, typical of me, I wrote and read a silly but heart-felt poem:

A toast to my much older sister,
A sister I miss very much
I know that you're watching and listening
And the family is here to get in touch.
John is happy he has found us
We are thrilled he found us, too,
Now Sophie has a brother and
That was thanks to you.
There are many things reminding us
Of you—too numerous to name
12 ears of corn and bacon
Are two of family fame.
So dearest sis, wherever you are,
Beside us or above,
Here's a tribute from your children
Made and given with so much love.

Carolyn yelled out. "I want some of that corn on the cob tonight."

"Great idea," Jack yelled.

"Okay then, let's go get some," Rick said, happy to have all that outward emotion over with.

I felt relief too. A tremendous emotional weight lifted. For John, for Sophie, for me, who somehow felt very responsible that this went well and that they liked, even loved, each other. I knew they did. They both had the same open heart and mind. They needed and wanted each other desperately.

*Attending Lind's memorial were: (back row) my brother
Rick Earle; John's son, John William; John Davis;
Merrick Earle; Anne Earle; (middle row) Rick's wife,
Cassandra; John's daughter Grace; Rick's daughter
Carolyn; (front row) Sophie; Carolyn's son, Jack;
Carolyn's daughter, Rozzie; and me. Don took the photo.*

Everyone hopped in their car—Sophie and John together, of course—and drove to our home in Charlotte. On the
way, Don and I stopped to pick up the fresh corn we decided we had to have after my poem and Carolyn's shout-out.

We had a wonderful night, all of us talking, smiling, and
happy.

My brother sat on the screened-in porch regaling Sophie and John with stories he could remember about Lind,

such as the time he, five, and Lind, seven, were on the front porch of their house on Marsh Street, and Lind had Rick take down his pants and show his "boy parts" to neighbors as they passed by.

According to Rick, Lind used to listen to *The Lone Ranger* program on the radio but wouldn't let Rick join her, instead pushing him from the room and shutting the door. When she joined a Lone Ranger fan club and received secret items in the mail, she bragged but wouldn't let him see.

"I was not smart enough or old enough to do those things on my own," Rick said.

One Sunday, Lind and Rick waited in the backyard, all dressed up for church, when Rick—baseball bat in tow—asked Lind to throw him the baseball. The bat bounced back from the ball and hit Rick in the middle of his forehead so hard it knocked him out. Lind, thinking she had killed him, ran screaming into the house. The family spent the morning in the emergency room rather than at church.

In addition to these "little brother" memories, Rick also shared more flattering stories of Lind, her being a cheerleader, being very popular in high school, and being a member of the National Honor Society.

He recalled a visit from her when he had just gotten out of the army and was starting back to work at Buffalo Forge in New York. Lind was on her way to Paris for the first time. He said she chose dinner at a French restaurant and was frustrated when she couldn't read the menu. She looked at Rick and said, "When I come back from this trip, I will be able to read this menu to you."

"It was a long time before she came back, even for a visit," he added.

The next morning the Davis family and Sophie headed for the beach, where Sophie swam in the ocean in her old, stretched bathing suit, trying, I hear, to hold the top up and not being very successful. Everyone laughed, including her. She and John took long walks on the beach, talking non-stop to catch up on all the years they hadn't known each other. They discovered they both had ear infections when they were young and some hearing loss in the same ear.

"I wish I had you as my brother growing up," Sophie told John.

"I wish I had been your brother then, too, Sophie."

"Well, next time we are together, we have to jump on the beds and have a pillow fight," Sophie laughed. "Since we never got to when we were younger."

"Absolutely." John gave her a big hug and kissed her on the head.

On John's back deck during Sophie's visit in July 2013: (back row) John's wife, Cami; John; me; (front row) Liza; Sophie; Grace; John William; and Henry, their sweet lab.

Sophie got a taste of everyday life with John and his family. I picked her up at the end of the week and then we drove back to Charlotte. She was heading back to France all too soon.

David confessed fear Sophie wouldn't return after meeting her brother, and she admitted that part of her didn't want to, but her life was with him, and she reassured him by phone several times. That fear was unwarranted, but eventually a braver, more independent, happier Sophie would ask him to move out.

John's wife later wrote:

> It was so special for John to find out he was conceived from two people who cared about each other deeply, etc., basically the knowledge that he was conceived in love and that he was wanted by his birth parents, and that there was a grandmother (Roz) out there thinking about him all those years. I could tell, watching him, he had constructed that myth in his head since he was 5 that his birth parents didn't want him, he was a throw away. I'm sure almost all adopted kids from those old days of the blind adoptions felt that way. And that, in some ways, shaped his personality a bit. So for me to see the myth crumble and reality take its place has been beautiful to watch. Sure, reality can and still is painful, but it's now his "real identity." Sometimes, it feels like it was destiny, or God's fingers all in it at the very least. All the people who made those hard decisions that messed up their own relationships going forward—Lind and her dad, Lind never

coming back home was probably really hard on your mom. They are all gone, except for Jim Rabon, and he was somewhat powerless, from what I see. Now, the people in the family who are left, maybe in a way, we have all helped heal a little piece of something that fractured them.

Sophie wrote to all of us when she arrived home:

Such a happy discombobulated David who lost his way. We made it in three hours instead of one and half!

    Furry shiny leany cats all over me

    I enjoyed and craved so for meeting yous all again and anew

      Bonnes journees!

      Your French sophie

And then she wrote at Christmas:

I love you all so much!

    Your frame [a small painting of mine] *hangs in the fire-oven room, and the little moon helps me every day, the path is long & mine seems mute and hidden sometimes… your book "eat pray love" I just finish. Has been my bible and will keep it around me.*

    I've opened xmas boxes this year and decorated a little, David likes it! We'll have flambé pudding at Scott's & Barbara on the 25th, this has become a ritual & I like it. But this year I'll miss you my biiig & heartyyyy family even more!

    I love you.

John copied me in on a written letter Sophie sent him in January:

Once upon a time…

Lind & Jean Paul married, telegrams come & I come & other telegrams come on this Friday 27th. I'm happy to look forward to longer days and the very fulfilled program of next year! This winter, David prepares his trip to Morocco in mid-February till end of March, with me flying to meet Nesha & the workshop. In between, D. cuts wood for the fire oven, and plays with colors & dying to make a label for the rugs. I play with the vacuum cleaner & dirt towels because I move around the kitchen & spider nests as well!! Hand sawing, reading, cooking, & hugging the cats are my most winter occupations, besides old Edmond [the older gentleman she took care of twice a week] *to go & nurse regularly—*

It's been a troubled period coming back from the States … back to daily couple life, & this couple of ours is, how to say? Like unfinished & the dynamic is very hard together. And I know this was because I could never find my place, neither geographically nor emotionally. To have met you has changed my roots & perspectives!! So again, a shaked autumn I spent, longing to get out of my "false" brain paths, long inscribed before my birth, and that I had built again and more.

The wall has cracked…

At last I may become a leaf in the water flow … a leaf comes from the tree, so much roots and branches and brother and sister leaves! To let me be in the flow of this life, I choose (horse, garden, man,

*animals, trees) and enjoy just what has to be done
… there's so much can't be bored & my imagina-
tion is always thinking,*

   I get near to happiness!!
   Thank you, John Brother
   All goodnesses to you & surroundings!
   Your eversophie

Scott emailed the day after they celebrated Sophie's for-
ty-seventh birthday that February:

*We had champagne, red wine, vegetarian pizza
with homegrown tomatoes, a homemade bûche de
Noël with chocolate and pears, delicious sweet and
sour pickles, local walnuts, music from the '60s to
the '80s, and a grand time.*

   *Sophie's haircut makes her look younger, but
there are also expressions that I don't think I've
seen before. She seemed very pleased with the occasion, in any event.*

Sophie wrote to John, June 17, 2014:

*"Can You Blame the Sky" song by Alela Diane.
That's a lovely song, just made for you, as "summer-
time" is for me, and thanks to you, brother, I do
open my wings, and it's amazing.*

And the next day she emailed John again:

*Just watched a movie called Secrets & Lies from
Mike Leigh, English filmmaker, about a girl looking
for her mother, can't say it's not touching. I had not*

*thought how courageous you had been looking for
your roots, and I hope you have achieved a path in
knowing us and your father. It has been a huge tremendous step forward to happiness for me. I never
allowed myself to be happy before, always breaking
down the chances life offered me, and it offered so
much! But the biggest chance is the gift you gave me
through allowing the truth to shine.*

*Mom was sick from the cries she didn't cry out.
I became sick from her sickness, now I may spread
my wings as the song says. I've stopped smoking
cannabis, it was my daily reason of waking up.
It gave me the little strength to still believe I was
worth something ... The days I had none were
terrible; I felt like hanging myself, thinking I was
ruining everything around me. I always had a mask
on, but could not stay long socializing, too hard to
wear a mask if you're not on stage.*

*Now that I know what happened, I feel so sorry
for Mom not trusting herself and me to tell the
truth. I want to thank you again and again.*

your little sis

My heart aches for Lind and Jim, Sophie and John—
for past hurts and secrets, which today might have been
avoided. I am, however, comforted knowing our family
has come together and loves each other deeply—nephews,
nieces, cousins, brother, and sister. Sophie and I needed to
be found by John as much as he needed to find us.

— 29 —

In October 2014, Don and I booked a river cruise from Switzerland to Amsterdam. We also set aside a few days before the trip to visit Sophie, as well as Lind's friend Scott, in the South of France. At that time, Sophie and David were still together. We drove from Montpellier to Béziers and then on to Saint-Pons-de-Thomières. Don and I exclaimed how beautiful the countryside was becoming as we

The road to Sophie's little hamlet, le Milieu (the middle village) goes right by her kitchen door.

got closer and closer to her home. Sophie's little village was mountainous and charming. The road past her house and into her hamlet was dirt and passed not two feet from her kitchen door.

Don and I were to stay the night in another old house, a very short walk from Sophie's house.

Sophie wrote:

it's a perfect little house, all set up and furniture by Marie, and cleaned up and decorated by me and D! You need nothing, there will be coffee and biscuits, shower towels and cozy rugs & blankets.

It was very rustic, all in stone inside and out. Sophie said Marie only used her home on vacation but did make it available for rent. The first floor had a monster fireplace that could have been where the family originally cooked their meals. We tried to use it since it was chilly in the house, but the fireplace did not draw very well and made the room too smokey. Even though there was a second floor there was only one small, though updated, bathroom on the first floor. The smallish kitchen was open to the living room and well stocked with everything we needed. Sophie had made it very special, with flowers and photos of family placed all around. The bedroom where we slept upstairs had one little electric light and mattress, both on the floor.

veggie soup, beetroot & carrot salad, panned pota-toes, all from the garden will await you at our place, from about 5 o'clock on. Don't forget warm clothes and rainshoes, autumn has set and nights are cold now.

David &/or I will be standing smiling! oh oh oh oh oh!

When we arrived, she was indeed smiling and jumping up and down. I am so happy we went. Now I can picture her, the house, her hamlet, her cats, her garden, her walk to Scott's house, whenever she writes me about goings on. We had a lovely lunch at Scott and Barbara's. Then Scott drove us to see other villages and hillside towns close by. Don and I had two fun-packed days, then headed up the Rhône River to Belfort, France, and took a train into Basel, Switzerland, to meet our river cruise.

After our trip, Sophie went through another rough patch. She told me the old man she sat for was not doing well and wouldn't live much longer. She needed to find another job. And she and David were not doing well. She asked him to move out, so he headed back to Morocco.

After a year, David came back to the village and rented a place nearby. It was hard for her to have him around. But he did bring in a small income by renting her greenhouse to have workshops on growing and dyeing indigo.

Our time with Sophie and the cruise were both wonderful. On the flight home, I thought a lot about how happy I was now that John found us and that he, his wife, and children are so loving and feel a real part of us. Just knowing that John is her brother, even if he is thousands of miles away, has given Sophie a new feeling of security. She was alone with her mother and father gone, but now she has a brother. She is braver, stronger, and has more energy to create and become her true joyful self. All of us are settling in and are ready to continue with our lives, with all the ups and downs, the pains and joys of having so many people to love.

POSTSCRIPT

As I write this in 2023, Sophie is well and happy. We spend more time catching up and sharing photos. Sophie quit her nursing job during the COVID pandemic and needed a way to make a little income. She had a few workshops in her home teaching friends English. Recently Sophie found out having a B&B in her home might prove more lucrative. Many bikers and hikers visiting her area may need a place to stay.

Her creative side shows in the close-up distorted photos she shares with us, which are like abstract art. She has learned about herbs and plants—which ones are edible, which ones can heal. She has meals with Scott and his dog, Iris, and spends time visiting with her girlfriends. Sophie also generously shares her land with her close neighbors for a community garden. I adore Sophie and am so proud of her. I really admire her and her way of living.

I received an email from Scott Griffith dated February 26, 2022, letting me know how he and the other two close friends of Lind's from Chapel Hill were getting along.

I don't "do" anything, that is to say I don't have a job and don't want one. I live on my pension. I've recently "lost" my wife to Alzheimer's and she's been taken to live with her daughter's family near London. I'm a bachelor now. I have a dog and lots to do tending a large house, cooking, ironing, hoovering, and, outside, tending to grass, roses, a kitchen garden, topiary, cutting wood, and so forth. I read and write whenever I can find time. My daughter lives and works in London and has two children, one who lives in London, the other in Barcelona. My son lives and works near Boston and has three boys, the youngest of whom is still in college. I, about to be 85, await the arrival of great-grandchildren.

Norton Tennille too is now retired, but fairly recently. He first practiced environmental law for many years in DC before moving to Cape Town in 1994. He founded and since then has volunteered for the nonprofit, SAEP, the South African Education and Environmental Project. He's married to Jane Keen, Director of SAEP. His lifelong passions are languages and literature, especially fiction and poetry, beginning with the ancient Greeks and Romans. He too reads and writes a lot.

Frank Nye is also retired and living in south Florida. He spends his time reading, seeing friends, and going to film and concerts.

All three of us correspond frequently, as we have done for many years, particularly since Lind's death. I'm the oldest, Lind was a month younger, then Frank, then Norton, the youngest, now over 80. And we all still refer frequently to Lind.

It's wonderful that these smart, loyal friends still think of Lind. They have given me rich memories that I will always cherish. Scott Griffith and Norton Tennille are still living, but Frank Nye passed away in December of 2022 after a brief illness. I will miss him.

Wyndham Robertson has been an incredible support and connection to the past and present for this story. She has also become a very good friend. She lives in Chapel Hill and is on the board of the Blanche & Julian Robertson Family Foundation, funded by her brother and named in memory of their parents. It is dedicated to improving the quality of life in Salisbury.

John provided me with his thoughts, and I include them here with his permission.

> *I have been blessed with a very positive reunification with both sides of my birth family. I am deeply grateful for the gift of their presence in my life. My birth father Jim, his loving wife Carol, and their children have been incredibly welcoming to me and my family. Unfortunately, my birth mother, Lind, passed away before I could find her. But luckily, I did find the rest of her family, who welcomed me with open arms. I'd like to think I've found pieces of my birth mother in all of her wonderful family.*
>
> *While the adoption cycle is certainly an emotional minefield for the birth parents, adoptive parents, and the adoptee, absolutely anything is possible with open, loving hearts. Because of my birth families'*

graciousness, much healing and closure has taken place for me. I am happy and eternally grateful for the many layers of my beautiful family, both my birth family and my adoptive family.

John's father Jim passed away in August of 2022 at the age of eighty-seven, but happily, Jim and his family and John and his family had twelve years to get to know each other.

As for Don, me, and our two boys, time has made quite a change in all our lives. Don and I are happily retired and have stayed busy through the pandemic and beyond: Don baking and playing golf; me painting and writing; our two grown sons settled, one studying Japanese and music, the other art and working as an expeditor in a restaurant. In January of 2019, we got our first dog, Echo, a golden doodle we call our grandson.

COVID isolation kept our French and American family apart for three years. The excitement of John finding us and Sophie meeting her brother has dimmed somewhat, yet we are comfortable knowing that we care about each other and are united as a family. And, of course, there is hope for a future reunion in France or America.

ACKNOWLEDGMENTS

I am so thankful to the following people. I could not have written this book without them.

My husband, Don, who was always saying, "Whatever it takes. Just finish the book!"

John Davis, whose quest to find his birth parents started me on this journey of discovering my sister.

Sophie Earle Coutou, my sister's daughter, who was terribly affected by her mom's illness and her parents' deaths and who found a sense of peace when she discovered she had a brother.

Gilda Morina Syverson, author of *My Father's Daughter* and my memoir teacher for many years, who assured me that this story was worth telling.

My fellow memoir class writers, who questioned, critiqued and always encouraged me.

Ann Campanella, author of *Motherhood: Lost and Found* and *Celiac Mom*, who provided great feedback.

Frank Nye, who was so generous and so honest in sharing his memories of my sister and his relationship with her.

Scott Griffith, Lind's longtime friend and now a neighbor and great friend to Sophie, who provided wonderful details.

Norton Tennille who sent me Dawn Potter's poem, which beautifully expressed his feelings about their lives in Chapel Hill.

Dawn Potter and Deerbrook Editions for allowing me to use her poem.

Other of my sister's friends who shared their thoughts about her with me: Jere Starling, Marjorie Starling, Brigitte Buire and Jennifer de Chabaneix.

Wyndham Robertson, who has followed Lind's story with enthusiasm and encouragement.

Robert Wilson III, Wyndham's friend, who helped me discover the name of a man who stood by Lind at a stressful time in her life.

The Children's Home Society post-adoption services, which shared information that had been previously sealed by law.

My big brother Rick, who regaled us with childhood stories I didn't know.

Nora Gaskin Esthimer, who edited and published this revised final memoir about my sister.

Kelly Prelipp Lojk, who copy edited and designed the book.

GENERAL BOOK CLUB QUESTIONS

1. What is the significance of the title? Did you find it meaningful?

2. What did you think of the writing style and content of the book? Did it keep you engaged?

3. Would the story have as much impact set in a different time period?

4. Were there any passages or quotes that stood out to you?

5. What did you like most about the book? What did you like the least?

6. How did the book make you feel? What emotions did it evoke?

7. What do you think the author's goal was in writing this book?

8. Is there a certain audience that should read this book?

9. Did your opinion of this book change as you read it? How?

10. Would you recommend the book to a friend? How would you summarize the story if you were to recommend it?

11. If you could talk to the author, what question would you want to ask?

12. What aspects of the story could you most relate to?

13. What songs or events were mentioned in the book? Did that help you understand the time period better?

14. Were you surprised by anything you read?

15. Was there anything not included that you wish had been?

www.ingramcontent.com/pod-product-compliance
Lightning Source LLC
Chambersburg PA
CBHW020239130626
46549CB00005B/1970